Parent to Parent

of related interest

Parenting a Child with Asperger Syndrome
200 Tips and Strategies
Brenda Boyd
ISBN 1 84310 137 8

Asperger's Syndrome
A Guide for Parents and Professionals
Tony Attwood
Foreword by Lorna Wing
ISBN 1 85302 577 1

Multicoloured Mayhem
Parenting the Many Shades of Adolescents and Children
with Autism, Asperger Syndrome and AD/HD
Jacqui Jackson
ISBN 1 84310 171 8

Understanding Autism Spectrum Disorders
Frequently Asked Questions
Diane Yapko
ISBN 1 84310 756 2

Can I tell you about Asperger Syndrome?
A Guide for Friends and Family
Jude Welton
Illustrated by Jane Telford
Foreword by Elizabeth Newson
ISBN 1 84310 206 4

What did you say? What do you mean?
An illustrated guide to understanding metaphors
Jude Welton
Illustrated by Jane Telford
Foreword by Elizabeth Newson
ISBN 1 84310 207 2

Freaks, Geeks and Asperger Syndrome
A User Guide to Adolescence
Luke Jackson
Foreword by Tony Attwood
ISBN 1 84310 098 3

Parent to Parent

Information and Inspiration
for Parents Dealing with Autism
or Asperger's Syndrome

Ann Boushéy

Jessica Kingsley Publishers
London and Philadelphia

First published in the United Kingdom in 2004
by Jessica Kingsley Publishers
116 Pentonville Road
London N1 9JB, England
and
400 Market Street, Suite 400
Philadelphia, PA 19106, USA

www.jkp.com

Copyright © Ann Boushéy 2004

Library of Congress Cataloging in Publication Data
Boushey, Ann, 1957-
  Parent to parent : information and inspiration for parents dealing with autism and Asperger's syndrome / Ann Boushey.
    p. cm.
Includes bibliographical references and indexes.
  ISBN 1-84310-774-0 (pbk.)
  1. Autism in children. 2. Autistic children--Care. 3. Parents of autistic children. I. Title.

RJ506.A9B68 2004
649'.154--dc22
                    2003026439

British Library Cataloguing in Publication Data
A CIP catalogue record for this book is available from the British Library

ISBN 1 84310 774 0

Printed and Bound in Great Britain by
Athenaeum Press, Gateshead, Tyne and Wear

This work is dedicated to my son who continues to inspire me, to Leland Zimmer who always believed in me, and to Shawn who continues to support me.

Acknowledgements

Acknowledgements need to go to Dr. Blackmon and Dr. Sodowsky for their close reading and honest opinions.

Disclaimer

This work is my story, my words and my opinion. It should in no way be taken as an expert's opinion. I am only an expert in *my* child's case.

Contents

You may give them your love but not your thoughts,
For they have their own thoughts.
You may house their bodies but not their souls,
For their souls dwell in the house of tomorrow,
which you cannot visit, not even in your dreams.
You may strive to be like them,
but seek not to make them like you.
For life goes not backward nor tarries with yesterday.
You are the bows for which your children as living arrows are
sent forth.

(Kahlil Gibran, The Prophet, *1923)*

Let me introduce myself

My son said the other day, "Mom, remember when I was little and I would tell people [in a robot voice] 'My name is Jon Boushéy. I live at 2045 Clark Drive in Hastings, Missouri. I go to Hastings Elementary and I'm in the 2nd grade.' Oh brother," he added. We both laughed, and as he went back to what he was doing, I began thinking about how far we've come. Here is my son, who doesn't yet understand the meaning of the word autism, but does understand that he used to speak in what is called *echolalia*—what he refers to as a robot voice. In second grade his speech teacher "scripted" introductions for him and took him around to greet people in the school. He got so good at it, of course had the scripts memorized, that he would then introduce himself in this way to grocery clerks, friends and even close relatives. Introductions were an important beginning for him, and introductions are important for me now.

If you and I were fellow parents at a school function, or if you were going to be working with my son in any way, I would say something along these lines: "I'm Ann Boushéy and this is my son, Jon. He's 14 now, and was given an educational diagnosis of high functioning autism at the end of his kindergarten year. We think he possibly has Asperger's Syndrome, but the two seem similar, and changing the diagnosis at this point would not change the help he is getting. He is our only child, and so far, he is doing just fine." Once this basic information was given, and you too introduced yourself, the subject may never come up again. It depends on each situation if I give any more details. But for this situation, I would like to give you much more than just the basics. I would like to tell you why I chose to write this book, give you some of its goals and explain a little about its format.

When I started thinking about putting this work together, I had to answer my own question: "Why another book on autism? Surely there are many books out there. What good would one more book be to anyone?" First of all, yes, there are many other books on autism out there. My purpose is not to replace them, but to add to them. In this book, I hope you will find information that you would not find in another book, along with information that has been gathered from many sources and now put together in one place, such as Chapter 2 on "The history of autism." One of my goals is to give you my take on this information, as a parent who has gone through, and continues to go through, what you too may be experiencing. What I have chosen to include is information that I wish had been in a book when my son was diagnosed years ago—information that I believe is important enough to pass on to other parents, and educators—and that may be considered "non-typical" on the subject of autism.

Mixed in with this information is also inspiration. It is true that no one understands what the parent of a disabled child goes through except another parent who is in the same situation. Keeping this in mind, I feel that sharing information is not the only thing we should be doing, but sharing inspiration too. When Jon was diagnosed, I could not find a book that, as it informed me, also worked to inspire me; hence my decision to combine the two. For closely tied to my goal of giving you information is the goal to let you know that you are not alone.

This statement has been used by an organization called MAAP (More Advanced Individuals with Autism, Asperger's Syndrome, and Pervasive Developmental Disorder/Not Otherwise Specified) since their inception: *You are not alone.* This knowledge is one of the most important things that you, as a parent, need to learn from this book, or any book that you read on autism. Whether your child has just been diagnosed, or you have been dealing with this diagnosis for a while, you are not alone in your struggles, frustrations, joys and successes. Many—too many—parents are going through the same experiences that you are going through. You do not have to "go it alone" unless you choose to.

But even if you choose to go it alone, you can become the expert when it comes to your child. In each chapter you will find references to books that helped me gain the knowledge to be the expert in my son's case. You too can do this. In the final chapters on different approaches and additional resources, you will find more information than you will probably be able to track down in a lifetime. Go after some of these resources. Please do read further. If you don't become the expert on your child, who will? Who loves your child enough to do so?

As you inform yourself, I believe that you will find what I found years ago: *knowledge brings peace of mind.* Yes, this knowledge sometimes upset me, confused me, or perhaps made me angry. But because I was no longer in the dark, I could have peace of mind while all of the other emotions were raging. To me, researching, studying and learning about autism is no different than making any decision in my life. If I'm going to buy a house, or a car, or take a trip, I am going to make an informed decision. I am going to study everything I can get my hands on before I make the decision, and I am going to stay up to date and keep reading long after the decision has been made. In this case, we are talking about your child. Why wouldn't you want to learn everything you can about his or her diagnosis?

Besides wanting to give other parents information and inspiration with this book, my other goal is to try to give autism a voice. If this were a book about a child who did not have an atypical diagnosis, I could possibly turn it over to that child to write it. There are recent books on autism spectrum disorders or Asperger's that have been written by these youngsters, or do have chapters written by an older child or young adult. But in my case, my child cannot write his own story. When he is older? Perhaps. But at the moment I am his voice, and thus autism's voice. I will have to tell you about my son because he doesn't have the words to do it himself. Not only do I feel this book will inform and inspire you, but in reading about my son's particular struggles and successes, you may see similarities to your child, and of course realize you are not alone.

Chicken nuggets for the soul

I'm sure many of us have read the now famous "Chicken Soup" books. I have found many of their short vignettes helpful and inspirational. In this book, however, you will find short pieces titled "Chicken Nuggets." However, this is not merely a play on words and, if I may misquote Hamlet, "There is a method in this madness" (my apologies to the Bard).

A few years back I attended a MAAP conference. I had previously been to several local conferences on autism, but this was the first I had attended that was on such a large scale. There were over 600 attendees trying to get to meetings and break-out sessions in a conference area that was set aside for perhaps 200. They had not expected such a turn-out. I was overwhelmed by the crowd, awed by the speakers and irrevocably changed by the time I went home. I made many connections with parents during the conference, and one woman in particular from Florida. We ended up eating all of our meals together and talked non-stop about our children—my son, her younger daughter. The last evening at dinner we began discussing our children's similarities and differences. We soon found out that although they were at different points on the autism spectrum, they were similar in that they both had hypersensitive hearing, aversions to certain clothing and were picky eaters. We both said at the same moment, "and he/she will only eat fried chicken." We paused, looked at each other, and then said in unison, "not white meat, dark meat only." Then our mouths dropped open and we laughed. What we both had thought was individual to our own child's quirkiness had to do with the autism. Something about the texture of the food in their mouths caused our children not to be able to eat stringy, white-meat chicken. We delved deeper into this subject and also found that, similarly, when they were much younger, both had practically lived on chicken nuggets. Whether they were chicken nuggets from a fast food restaurant, or the pre-breaded frozen kind from the grocery store, this had been their food staple, until they had gotten a little older and begun eating fried chicken—dark meat only.

This of course wasn't the only thing I learned from this conference, but it was an important point for me. What I learned from this simple conversation with this mom was that my autistic child was very similar to other autistic children. His food issue, something that I had always felt was somehow my fault because I didn't force him to "eat what was put in front of him" was typical of an autistic child. Not only was his picky eating related to texture and autism, but his food choice of chicken nuggets seemed related too. Suddenly I felt that my atypical child was typical. He lived on a very small food group along with a multivitamin, and this was typical. What a feeling of "relief" this information gave me, that other parents out there were going through the same battles that I was—right down to the chicken nuggets!

In addition to chicken nuggets, one of my favorite English writers, Virginia Woolf, points out that "the first duty of a lecturer [or writer] is to hand you after an hour's discourse a nugget of pure truth to wrap up between the pages of your notebooks and keep on the mantelpiece for ever" (1957, p.4). A nugget of pure truth: something the writer says that pings with you, so that you take it away with you, mull it over, and refer back to it from time to time. Woolf, of course, is speaking of gold nuggets, and we find many in her works. However, in this book, my nuggets are chicken—short illustrations that I hope you, the reader, will be able to find in them something that inspires and supports you. One conversation about chicken nuggets changed my whole way of thinking about my child. I have hopes that in these nuggets you will also find something just as beneficial.

References

Woolf, V. (1957) *A Room of One's Own.* San Diego: Harcourt Brace.

Chapter One

The grief cycle
One parent's trip around

I have read that the two most stressful events in one's life are divorce and the death of a loved one. According to a survey from the National Center for Health Statistics (2001), the divorce rate is 4.2 divorces per 1000 population per year, and death and mortality rate charts tell us that almost every American will experience the death of a close family member in his or her lifetime. But I believe that there is a third event just as distressing and devastating as divorce and death. It is only coincidental that this word also begins with a *d*. The word is *disability*. Having a child with a disability is every parent's nightmare. About one in five Americans have some kind of disability. Most people read these statistics, nod their heads, and move on to the next article. But what happens when one of these three events affects us personally? What happens when the divorce is our own, the death is someone close to us, the disability affects our child? There is another link among these three events and this link is not coincidental: we grieve.

The grief cycle is a natural process of the human condition. Psychologists have been aware of this for a long time when death is involved. Almost every book about death and dying touches on the cycle in some way. When a loved one dies, you grieve, and a pattern can be found in this grief. In the same way, within the last two decades, books on divorce have also used this cycle to explain what a person goes through during a divorce. Hence divorce and death are additionally linked by the way we react to both events.

As a parent of a child with a disability, I have come to realize that grief is grief. A small life-changing book titled *Crossing Bridges: A Parent's Perspective on Coping After a Child is Diagnosed with Autism/PDD* brought this fact home (Campbell, Peerenboom and Satkiewicz-Gayhardt 1996). The grief cycle is the same whether you are talking about a divorce, a death, or a disability. The US census report states: "Disability is no respecter of age, sex or race. Even among children ages 6 to 14, about 1 in 8 have some type of disability" (US Department of Commerce 1997, par.4). Do people even listen when they hear these statistics? I know that I didn't. It wasn't until I was told "Your child is autistic" that I listened. But first I did what every person does when dealing with an episode so distressing and devastating; so similar to divorce and death: I grieved.

Whether I wanted to or not, I went through the cycle. Because no two people are exactly the same, everyone goes through it differently, and it doesn't matter what the diagnosis is. Some people will skip parts of this cycle, some will spend different lengths of time at different points. But we all begin at the same point, and that point is our reaction to our child's diagnosis.

Shock

I have heard some parents say when referring to their child with a disability, "I always suspected something" or "I was glad to get my feelings finally confirmed." This was not the case in our family. Our son was our firstborn and only child. By our way of thinking, he had a typically "normal" development. He met all of his early milestones—first words, walking, growth. With hindsight, I can say that his language did not develop as rapidly as normal. But we are a bilingual family. My son grew up with my mother-in-law as his secondary caregiver. As he developed, he heard two languages, and his first words included words in both languages. We were told by our family doctor that some speech delays were normal in a bilingual household because the child doesn't know which language to respond in. Another important milestone was reached at the early age of five, when my son began reading. At first we thought that he had just memorized the Dr. Seuss books, but soon we realized he was actually sounding out and reading new words. At his kindergarten screening I remember being told that they couldn't get him to stop talking long enough to test him. It took them an hour to discover his skills while trying to distract him from what he wanted to talk about. At that time, I think his interests were *Sesame Street* and dinosaurs. When he entered kindergarten, there was one other clue that could have tipped us off if we had known any better: he had hypersensitive hearing. We had to leave a circus right after it started because of the cannon shot. We had to leave a live performance of *Sesame Street* because the music was too loud. He wouldn't just become upset, he would become terrified and inconsolable. So we took him to have his hearing tested and the audiologist said he had 10 percent greater hearing than a normal child.

Armed with the audiologist's report and pre-kindergarten scores stating that he could already read, he entered school and had a disastrous first semester. He was not functioning at all well in the classroom, and they couldn't get him to go into the gymnasium—we thought because of the echoes. I tackled the gym problem by going up to the school every time his class was in PE and slowly working him into the gym. It took us two months, but by November he was in the gym with his class. The school handled the classroom problems by moving him into a different classroom with a very structured teacher and an entirely different atmosphere. He improved 100 percent in this new environment, but still they wanted to test him to see if they were missing something.

In May, two weeks before school ended, we were asked to attend a meeting to hear the test results. In my own mind, I thought I knew what to expect. I told my husband that I believed they were going to try to tell me that our son had attention deficit disorder (ADD). I had looked up information on ADD and knew that with his attention span and ability to sit and read books or focus on a toy for hours at a time, he did not have ADD. My husband and I met with 12 educators. One of them was an autism consultant brought in by the school district. I think it was the moment she was introduced to me that shock began. The meeting lasted more than two hours. The Individualized Education Plan (IEP), which included the test results and a plan for next year, was more than 14 pages long. The words I will never forget were, "Yes, we know your son began reading at the age of five, but he shows definite autistic-like behaviors." Shock. As an undergraduate, I'd had a few classes in early childhood education. They said the word autism and I had a mental picture of a small child rocking in the corner of a room, on his face, a blank stare. Shock. It's the same when you hear of a loved one dying, or when your spouse tells you he or she wants a divorce. Things become blurry after the devastating news. You continue to function, but you don't know how you do it or later remember the details. I did sign the IEP, but I wrote along the margin that I did not agree with their diagnosis and was signing only because my son had problems and needed help. Thank goodness the special service director had the intelligence not to push the point at this time. She had been there before. She was very familiar with the symptoms of parental shock. What did we do next? We got up and went home.

Denial

Next on the cycle is depression. But for me, I went straight to denial. My denial began when I was still sitting at that table and I wrote on the IEP that I did not agree with their diagnosis. School ended and I spent the next two months in denial. But it's amazing how denial works, or rather doesn't work. Reality just has a way of slapping you in the face and waking you up. My wake-up call happened in August.

My son and I traveled to St. Louis to visit family and to go to the Six Flags amusement park. The day before going to the park, we visited our favorite bookstore. While my son was two aisles over in the children's section, I found myself drawn to the education/disabilities section. I picked up a book written for parents of children "newly diagnosed" with autism, looked at the cover, put the book back, and went to check on my child. A few minutes later, I went back to the same shelf and pulled the same book off the shelf. I opened it up and saw that it was written in a "ten most frequently asked questions" format. I couldn't stop myself. I read the entire book from cover to cover while my son was two aisles away reading to his heart's content. The book was a paperback, 250 pages or so, and I remember being in that bookstore for a long time. Reality dawned. This book was talking about my son: from obsessive-compulsiveness, to perseveration (insistence) on one subject, echo-like speech, and his lack of interest socially—even his sensitive hearing and the fact that he was hyperlexic (started reading early). He was there, described between the covers of a book. I began to cry and went over to the children's section. I sat down on the floor a short distance from my little boy and watched as he read. I cried some more. I had walked 20 steps from one bookshelf to the other and had come away a changed person. I would never be the person that I was before I had read that book. I would never look at my child in the same way. This book was telling me that my child had a disability. He wasn't just unique or quirky, he was impaired, disabled—damaged.

Although my understanding of my child had drastically changed, my child was still the same. We went to Six Flags the next day and had a wonderful time. My son didn't understand why Mommy would look at him and sometimes cry. He was too busy riding the roller coaster, eating a kid's chicken nugget meal (his main food group at the time), or talking about his favorite video and repeating it word for word. We took snapshots in a photo booth—the kind that shoots a strip of black and white photos in five minutes. We laughed and both made goofy faces. I will always look at those pictures and remember that this was the time when I realized my son was autistic. We had so much fun together, even while reality was dawning.

A mixed bag

I've grouped the next part of the grief cycle together. These are the "feelings" that you go through—guilt, shame, isolation—and here is where I also went through my depression. I came back from our trip carrying most of these feelings on my shoulders. I called the school and told the services director that I now agreed with their diagnosis, but needed more information. They put me in touch with a local organization for autism. During the next month, I visited their office numerous times, received at least 15 packets of information, and checked out books from their library. Also during this time, I cried at the drop of a hat, especially when I was sitting and watching my child. When this depression eased up a bit, I began to read to find the reason for his autism. This is where a new emotion set in.

Guilt

This was not a new feeling to me. After all, I was a mom and most moms feel guilt at some time over their children: "I should be doing this, I could have done that." But this was a new form of mommy guilt. This guilt was the feeling that I had done something during pregnancy or during the developmental years of my child's life that had caused his autism. This is why I read to find the reason for autism. Imagine my surprise when I read that they hadn't found the exact reason. However, the new findings, since 1990, did conclusively state one thing: it is no longer believed that children with autism are this way because of lack of affection from their mothers. The "refrigerator mom" explanation had been put to rest when they realized that autism is a neurological disorder. The experts now believe that autism is an abnormal fetal development, through no fault of the mother. Did this put my guilt to rest? Yes, no, maybe, but sometimes not. Something the experts on grief seldom tell you is that you can continue through parts of this cycle for the rest of your life. Grief over death, divorce, disability is with you for life and you can revisit points on the cycle when you least expect it. Guilt is one of those first emotions that at times rears its ugly head in my life.

Isolation

Isolation is another one that crops up regularly. I now had an extra burden of care placed on my shoulders. I was not only a mother with the normal cares and worries of a mother, but I was a mother of a child with a disability. No one could understand what I was going through except another mom of a child with a disability. The world suddenly became a very small, narrow universe. My child was disabled. He had no interest in relating to other kids and their activities, so how could I relate to other moms? I tried. We participated in T-ball. But it was hard to explain to the other parents, whom you had just met, why you were there for only the practices and not for the games because your son didn't understand the concept of a game, or of competition. This was a time when connecting with other parents of children with autism became very important to me. I remember calling a woman, whose name I had gotten from another woman, who knew that this woman had a 20-year-old daughter with autism. Just that one-hour phone call to a total stranger was the lifeline that I needed to pull me from my quagmire of feelings. But after I pulled myself out, I immediately panicked. I remember wondering if it was too late to help my son. I remember becoming almost manic in my need to know more.

Panic

But no matter how much I read on the subject, I felt behind. No matter how many conferences on autism that I attended, it wasn't enough. My son was growing up right before my eyes and I felt that for every step he took forward, I needed to take two to stay caught up. I'm sure other parents of "normal" children feel this way at times, but with a disability it is magnified a million times over. He was doing well in the general education classroom with an aide, speech therapy, and occupational therapy. In speech, the therapist worked with him on those (now) famous first "scripted" conversations, trying to get him to learn first by rote how to communicate with someone else. In occupational therapy, they begin with his sense of where his body is in space, in technical terms referred to as *proprioception*. But in my terms, he had trouble walking through doors without hitting the doorframe because he had no knowledge of where his body was in relationship to other things and people. My husband and I met with the IEP team every two weeks so we could stay on top of things, and it was at these meetings that I shared my new-found knowledge with the educators. I'm sure now that a lot of it was not new to them. But some of it was, and they were just as enthusiastic as I to learn everything we ever wanted to know about high functioning autism, but never thought to ask. It wasn't until later on that I found out that my son was the first child in their school diagnosed with high functioning autism. They were enthusiastic because this was all new to them too, and they sincerely wished to make a difference in my son's life. The more knowledge I acquired on the subject, the less panic I felt. I still believe to this day that in my case knowledge brought peace. Perhaps because I was so caught up with my quest for knowledge, I didn't go through the anger or bargaining part of the grief cycle.

Anger

You are angry at the world, yourself, your spouse, perhaps even at God. Many parents go through this when their child is diagnosed, because life is not fair. I wasn't angry, maybe because sometime during my life I had already learned that life was not fair, and there was no one to blame for this fact. My child was autistic and being angry would not change anything. However, now that I think about it, maybe I was angry a little. I do remember ranting and raving at my loving spouse over little things like taking the trash out or leaving his dirty socks in the middle of the floor. Thank goodness he was the calm one and realized that it was the IEP meeting we had just attended that had brought this on. A wondrous thing about loved ones: they love us in spite of our anger.

Bargaining

Many people make bargains with themselves, consciously or subconsciously. If I do everything, try every cure, then this will go away. If I change his diet, try a different educational method, then he will be fine. This is another very normal reaction for a parent. I think it was the reading I did that kept me from making these bargains. In my reading, I read not only that autism is a neurological disorder in the way a child's brain has developed, but also that it is not curable. Once your child is autistic, he will always be autistic. The *symptoms* of autism can diminish with early intervention, and teaching the child ways to function in the real world is the goal. But my quirky little boy will always be quirky. Even now at the age of 12 when he hugs someone, he smells their perfume. At night, when he hugs me before he goes to bed, he is smelling my "after shower smell." Thus, this causes me to wonder whether he is hugging me because he enjoys the affection of a hug, or because he only enjoys my smell. Of course, watch out if it is a smell he doesn't like, because he will definitely tell you!

Acceptance and hope

Once I realized this key, I moved on to the next step in the cycle. Acceptance and hope—the two go together. Yes, I accept that my child has autism and will always have autism, but that doesn't mean we are without hope. One of the things I learned in the early days of kindergarten when he was having terrible, horrible, unhappy days was to focus on the positive. I remember too many days when I would arrive at the school to pick him up, and he would be lying somewhere on the floor, usually face down. His teacher would explain that he'd had a pretty good day up to a little while ago, when he had gotten upset about something and had "shut down." On the way home I would have conversations with myself. Okay, he has autism, but let me tell you what he can do. He can remember a Walt Disney video almost word for word and even do the different voices; therefore he can look at a spelling list and have the words memorized after one reading. He can tell you when a certain movie came out at the theaters—day of the week, date, and year. Consequently, he is great at mental math, long division, and multiplication. We don't ask him how he does it. He just does it. He learns visually and thinks in pictures, not in generalities and concepts like we do. Hence, if he hasn't seen it before he will not have that information stored on his "hard disk." The more information he puts in, the more he can spit out. He is just like a walking computer. At every IEP meeting we try to emphasize the positive things he can do.

The main thing I have learned by studying the grief cycle and applying it to my own life is that I am a normal parent who had normal reactions when told that my child had a disability. As I mentioned before, there are times when the steps on this cycle come back to haunt me—thoughts of guilt, feelings of isolation, depression. This, too, is normal. After the death of a loved one there is still grief at certain times in one's life. Thinking about a devastating divorce will also bring on moments of grief. So, too, will a disability. But the last step in the cycle lasts forever as well, acceptance and hope. I may have changed greatly during this trip through the cycle, but did my child change? No. He is still my beautiful, firstborn, and only child, who just happens to have autism.

References

Campbell, R., Peerenboom, B. and Satkiewicz-Gayhardt, V. (1996) *Crossing Bridges: A Parent's Perspective on Coping After a Child is Diagnosed with Autism/PDD*. New Jersey: PUP Foundation.

National Center for Health Statistics (2001) *Monthly Vital Statistics Report 47*, 21, 10 July. www.cdc.gov/nchs/fastats/divorce.html (2002, Jan. 4).

US Department of Commerce (1997) *Census Brief*, December 1997. (CENBR/97–5).

www.census.gov/prod/3/97pubs/cenbr975.pdf (2002, Jan. 4).

chicken nugget # 1

Focusing on the positive

Welcome to Holland

I am often asked to describe the experience of raising a child with a disability—to try to help people who have not shared that unique experience to understand it, to imagine how it would feel. It's like this… When you are going to have a baby, it's like planning a fabulous vacation trip—to Italy. You buy a bunch of guide books and make wonderful plans. The Coliseum. The Michelangelo David. The gondolas in Venice. You may learn some handy phrases in Italian. It's all very exciting.

After months of eager anticipation, the day finally arrives. You pack your bags and off you go. Several hours later, the plane lands. The stewardess comes in and says, "Welcome to Holland."

"*Holland*?!!" you say. "What do you mean Holland?? I signed up for Italy! I'm supposed to be in Italy. All my life I've dreamed of going to Italy."

But there's been a change in the flight plan. They've landed in Holland and there you must stay.

The important things is that they haven't taken you to a horrible, disgusting, filthy place full of pestilence, famine and disease. It's just a different place.

So you must go out and buy new guide books. And you must learn a whole new language. And you will meet a whole new group of people you would never have met.

It's just a *different* place. It's slower-paced than Italy, less flashy than Italy. But after you've been there for a while and you catch your breath, you look around…and you begin to notice that

Holland has windmills…and Holland has tulips. Holland even has Rembrandts.

But everyone you know is busy coming and going from Italy…and they're all bragging about what a wonderful time they had there. And for the rest of your life, you will say, "Yes, that's where I was supposed to go. That's what I had planned."

And the pain of that will never, ever, ever, ever go away… because the loss of that dream is a very very significant loss.

But…if you spend your life mourning the fact that you didn't get to Italy, you may never be free to enjoy the very special, the very lovely things…about Holland.

(Emily Perl Kingsley 1987)

Afterthought

When I contacted Ms. Kingsley seeking permission to place her poem in my book, I was finally able to track her home number down through information. I called her one Sunday morning, saying when she answered the phone, "Is this Emily Kingsley, the writer?" Now some people may be tempted to hang up at this point. Obviously I wasn't someone she knew, but Emily didn't. She very graciously listened as I told her I was a mom who was publishing a book, and was seeking permission to include her poem.

Then she did something that only parents do, who share this common ground called disability. She spoke to me like I was an old friend, got excited for my book and asked how my son was doing. And there, on a Sunday afternoon across long-distance phone lines, another bond was made with a total stranger, and not only a stranger, but someone who has won Emmys, who writes for television, and has received more awards than I can count on two hands. She shared with me that her son was now 30 years old, living with a few friends in their own apartment, and with only part time support. She told me about her son's book, *Count Us In, Growing Up with Down Syndrome*, written entirely by Jason and his friend Mitchell Levitz, which also received awards. And in that short conversation, we were just moms talking about our children, mine reaching the terrible teenage years and hers grown up and on his own. But because of this thing called disability (it didn't matter that the disabilities were different), we were able to connect and speak parent to parent, mom to mom. Because you see, it doesn't matter that she is a famous writer, or that our sons' disabilities are different, we are moms and we are both living daily in Holland.

I read the previous piece on *Holland* right after my son's diagnosis, and I copied it and carried it around with me for years after. This is exactly what it is like. My husband and I had other plans for our son, and our plans had not included autism. Hence, after we had grieved for the country we didn't end up in, and had moved closer to acceptance and hope, we still had to come to grips with this "new country" that we were suddenly presented with. The first thing we had to learn was, yes, it is a different place, but who said it is all bad?

Parents of "neurotypical" children have to focus on the positive in their child's life, and with an "atypical" child, we realized how much more important this was. Every time I attend an IEP meeting (and in the early days they were every two weeks), I try to end the meeting by asking about the progress that my child is making. Not only does this help us, but this reminds the educators and professionals at the meeting that my child really is a success story. And not just "big" successes like being able to function in a regular classroom with an aide up until the fifth grade (sixth grade he was without the aide), but "small" successes as well.

When Jon was ten years old, he was so excited that he had finally learned how to tie his tennis shoes by himself. Before that, we had searched long and lengthily for tennis shoes with Velcro fasteners in his size. (Now of course, you can find them in adult sizes.) But I'll never forget his joy over this achievement; not notable to some parents, but to us a milestone.

Just recently he and his dad and I were sitting on the couch watching a basketball game, and Jon, who is "in and out" when it comes to paying attention to something he's not interested in, suddenly yelled "Hey, Mom, listen!" I leaned closer and heard a quiet snap of his fingers. "I've learned how to snap," he exclaimed. My husband and I stopped watching the game, and we all began snapping our fingers. Sure enough, we could hear his quiet finger snaps along with ours. "Now I have to learn how to whistle!" he informed us.

Shoe tying, snapping his fingers, and whistling, these are some of my son's successes and goals. Do I forget that at his present age of 12 he still won't go into a theater and watch a music show because of the dark, and the loud music? No. Or that he still gets very upset and bursts into tears when a glass of something spills? Unfortunately, no. But among the many challenges are the sometimes small successes. These are what we parents need to remember and try to focus on.

It's not what our children can't do, it is what they can. Yes, autism is a different country, but it still has its good points. Because of my son's amazing memory, the music director allowed him to be the "MC" for their spring musical called *Family Feud*. Jon sat at a podium in front of an auditorium full of parents, with 200 fellow fourth graders singing behind him. He smiled and hammed it up, and thoroughly enjoyed introducing the acts and MC-ing the show.

Also, he may have trouble understanding if someone is taking advantage of him, but because of his autism he is polite and gentle with others and doesn't have a mean bone in his body.

A verse from a song by Enya constantly runs through my mind: "On my way home I remember only good days. On my way home I can remember only best days." As parents, we must remember the good days because in the country of autism there may be too many bad ones. In our case, it seems that my son has three good weeks and one bad, so it feels as if we are constantly taking three steps forward and one step back. But at least we can take those three steps, no matter how small they may seem. No, we didn't plan on being in this country. But if we don't make the best of it and focus on the good points, we will miss them. And in doing so we may completely miss out on our son's life.

Chapter Two

The history of autism

Is there a problem?

Picture a room full of preschoolers, ages three to five. It is morning work time and they are coloring a worksheet on the letter A. One little boy, who looks to be about five, has caught your attention. He is very studiously coloring, but unlike the other children has not once spoken during the activity. The other children are digging in the boxes of crayons, fighting over colors, chattering to each other or about their pictures. But this little boy doesn't say a word. Silently he colors, searches in the box for his next crayon, then sits or kneels back down on his chair. Although he is quiet, he seems to be happy, and you wonder if he is "non-verbal." Looking over his shoulder, you see that he has colored the letter A in a rainbow of colors, each small section of the letter a different color. Now he is doing the objects, apple, ant, and alligator, also in the same rainbow of color. If you look a little closer, you may notice that he is going through the box of colors in the order that they are placed in the box. If one of the children inadvertently places a crayon back in the box in the wrong order, he patiently takes the time to rearrange them back into an order that only he is aware of.

After a few minutes the teacher claps her hands to tell the children that it is circle time. All of the children quickly stop what they are doing and run to sit on a red circle on the floor. The boy looks up and becomes agitated. He cries, "Wait! Wait!" and you realize for the first time that he is verbal. He becomes more upset, and the teacher explains that it is circle time and he can finish the picture later. He pulls away from the teacher's gentle touch on his shoulder, and throws himself onto the floor on his stomach, his face pressed into the floor, eyes closed. The teacher tries to persuade him to join the circle, but he doesn't respond to her, so she joins the circle and begins the lesson. As she reads a story, he continues to lie rigidly on the floor.

Halfway through the story, he moves to a sitting position. He glances once in the teacher's direction as she holds up the book, and then he focuses his gaze out the windows. During the rest of story, he sits alone, his gaze fixed out of the windows almost in a catatonic state. As the teacher finishes the story, the bell rings for recess. All of the children eagerly jump up to get their jackets, but this little boy doesn't move. When the teacher approaches him and touches his shoulder, he flinches as if she has hurt him. She tells him to get his jacket and line up for recess. He does as he is asked, and as the other kids jostle for position in line, he is still standing at the coat rack. He has his jacket on and you notice that he seems to be talking to himself. By now, all of the other children are in line except him. The teacher calls to him to please line up. He lines up and continues talking to himself in a quiet voice. As they troop out to recess, you follow along behind him, and wonder if the boy is talking to an imaginary playmate or singing a song.

Out on the playground the other children run off to play. But this boy stays at the edge of the playground by himself and steps up onto the railroad ties that mark the perimeter of the playground. He begins walking on the ties around the playground, and for the full 20 minutes of recess, this is what he does—around and around. At no time does he play with another child, approach another child or even seem aware of the other activity on the playground. He is smiling and talking to himself and seems to be having a great time walking and balancing along the ties. At one point a ball gets in his path. The boy stops and waits until the owner retrieves it, and when the other child says something to him, he doesn't respond.

When the teacher blows the whistle for the children to go inside, this little boy is standing nearby. At the sound of the whistle he quickly puts his hands over his ears and cringes. As the other children noisily line up, he stands in their midst, with his hands covering his ears. Not until the noise subsides does he join them at the end of the line. They stand in place as the teacher gives them instructions about lining up quietly and quickly. All of the children are facing forward in the line and listening, but this little boy is facing in the opposite direction. However, he seems to have been paying attention, because when the line moves to go inside, he turns and follows.

To the observer, it becomes evident that these are probably not normal behaviors for a five-year-old: lack of social awareness or any interest in interaction with others; very limited verbal skills, and none socially; throwing a tantrum and then shutting down when something happens that he doesn't like; hypersensitive hearing; hypersensitive to touch; staring at objects almost in a catatonic state; and carrying on a constant conversation with himself that seems meaningless to others. Yet he displays advanced learning skills in early math and has begun reading before the others have. His abilities on the computer are also advanced for his young age. Thus, there is a definite gap between social and academic skills. The child will probably be tested to see if anything is wrong, and after a battery of tests, the answer may come as a surprise. The diagnosis for this little boy is "autism, or autistic-like." Where does the observer go next?

> The farther back you can look, the farther forward you are
> likely to see.
>
> *(Winston Churchill)*

Where does one start?

In most cases, when someone wishes to study a particular subject he or she delves into the history. But in this case, in studying autism, I was told not to read anything prior to 1970 and advised not to rely on autism's history. Some specialists in the field will also tell parents to read only the most current information—approximately 1990 to the present. Does this mean that this disorder has been detected only in the last ten years? No. But if you were to go back further and look at the history of autism, you will find that in the past 50 years the definition of autism has drastically changed from childhood schizophrenia to a developmental neurological disorder. As a result, the treatment of autism has also drastically changed.

Hence, I did what was suggested to me. I started with the present information on autism and worked my way backwards to about 1990. Once I had a grasp on the basic definition and behaviors, current interventions, and immediate resources, I felt a little more informed. For some as yet unexplained reason, my child had a neurological disorder that caused him to display certain behaviors and impaired him socially and cognitively. We quickly put into place measures to help him in the regular classroom, which included a para professional (aide) and had him pulled during the week for speech and occupational therapy. I also located places for me to get more information or help as needed.

But once this was all set up and as the school years progressed, I felt like there was a gap in my education on autism. When we were students and were researching a subject, didn't we start at the beginning? If the topic was the space program, didn't we go back to look at how the space program developed through the years? What about if we were diagnosed with breast cancer? Wouldn't we read everything we could get our hands on that even mentioned breast cancer, the history of the disease and its treatment? It felt odd to me that I would avoid an entire era of information on a subject that had so irrevocably changed my family's life. Thus, I went back. I went back to the beginning and read everything that I could find about the history of autism.

The purpose of this chapter is to share that information with you. Think of this history as a grafted-in family history. You and I didn't want to have anything to do with it, but it is there, and now a part of our family life. Churchill said, if I may paraphrase his words: If we want to understand our future, we must understand our past.

Important beginnings—1940

It helped me if I compared the progression of the definition of autism to preparing a meal. First you put the main dish on the stove and bring it to a boil. Then you busily prepare the side dishes, allowing the main dish to simmer, until you finally place the completed meal on the table. This history is of course not all inclusive, but this is the research that helped me. Thus, in the early days of the 1940s, the dish was first placed on the stove.

In 1943 Leo Kanner wrote a report titled "Autistic Disturbances of Affective Contact." He reported on 11 children "whose condition differs so markedly and uniquely from anything reported so far" that he hoped it would lead to "a detailed consideration of its fascinating peculiarities." Several of these children were brought to him and introduced as "imbeciles", "idiots"or "schizophrenic" (pp.217–242). By observation, he proved that this was incorrect. He noted that these children kept to themselves, enjoyed only their own company, and had very little interest in the world going on around them. He detailed their strained relationships with their family and their lack of interest in peers. A few of these children were non-verbal and remained that way, but several of them developed a type of communication, if not considered social communication. After tracking these 11 children for several years, and being in close communication with their parents, Kanner comes to the conclusion that "these characteristics form[ed] a unique syndrome more frequent than is indicated by the paucity of observed cases," and adds that the "fundamental disorder is the children's inability to relate themselves in the ordinary way to people and situations from the beginning of life" (p.242). Not only is Kanner credited with possibly conducting the first case studies of this condition, but here, at the very beginning, is where a distinguishing ingredient is thrown into our pot. Kanner states that these children displayed an "extreme *autistic* aloneness" (p.242, my emphasis). As Michael Rutter states, confusion began in the very beginning. Autism was the term that Bleuler had used in the years 1911 to 1950 in referring to "the active withdrawal into fantasy shown by schizophrenic patients" (Rutter 1978, p.139). In fact, well into the 1970s the World Health Organization (WHO) used this term in its definition of schizophrenia: "a disturbed perception, abnormal affect out of keeping with the real situation and *autism*" (Rutter 1972, p.321, my emphasis).

However, Kanner didn't stop with these preliminary observations. He specifically states in his report that "this [condition] is not, as in schizophrenic children or adults, a *departure* from an initially present relationship; it is not a *withdrawal* from formerly existing participation" (1943, p.242, my emphasis), meaning according to Kanner, there was not a gradual change in the children's conditions, but this "aloneness" was evident from the beginning (p.248). Unfortunately however, the damage had already been done, and the confusion began. Kanner's autism was immediately connected to the autism associated with schizophrenia. Approximately a year later the term "infantile autism" was also coined and used by professionals in the field; "infantile" referring to the age of onset in the child. In addition the term "childhood schizophrenia" was used interchangeably with "infantile autism" (Kanner 1971, p.140).

If this was the first definition of this disorder, what was the treatment for these children at that time? In 1970 Kanner followed up on the 11 children's progress and treatment. Out of his 11 case studies, one child they could not track down because the mother refused follow-up treatment and dropped out of sight, and another was taken out of treatment into seclusion with his mother, and not trackable. Seven of the children were placed into group homes or state mental hospitals, resulting in only two left living in a normal setting. These two went on to lead successful if somewhat "assisted" lives (Kanner 1971, p.142). Thus, the treatment for the majority of these children was to institutionalize them. In his article, Kanner vividly points out that these institutionalized children quickly lost their "luster" after admission:

> Originally fighting for their aloneness…struggling for the status quo, originally astounding the observer with their phenomenal feats of memory, they yielded readily to the uninterrupted self-isolation and soon settled down in a life not too remote from a nirvana-like existence. (Rutter 1971, p.143).

He also notes that all of their previous IQ scores dropped down to what he referred to as "low-grade moron or imbecile" (p.143). He concludes that this was not treatment but containment, a sentence of isolation. He ends his report by wondering if a different treatment other than state hospitals would have brought a better outcome in all of the patients, or whether it was the individuals themselves and the progression of their different conditions that affected the final outcome.

Continuing research—1940 to 1960s

Now that the dish was on the stove, it began to simmer. During approximately the next 20 years "early infantile autism/childhood schizophrenia" was closely scrutinized. Kanner's definition was looked at, picked apart, looked at again, and argued about. But in spite of all of this scrutiny, it didn't drastically change in any way. This disorder was considered a mental illness—psychosis—and according to Milt (1963) there was "a growing belief that childhood schizophrenia is not really a single disease but actually a number of different kinds of mental illnesses of childhood having similar symptoms." At this time, the specialists also began to speak of this condition as "childhood schizophren*ias*" (Milt 1963, p.4, my emphasis). Hence, at this point they were trying to press these numerous diseases with "similar symptoms" into the mold of schizophrenia.

Consequently, because the definition basically remained unchanged, during the next 20 years the treatment of early infantile autism/childhood schizophrenia also remained unchanged. In Milt's (1963) pamphlet on mental illnesses in children, Carl Fenichel, director of a school for mentally ill children, is quoted as saying: "At our school are the silent ones who stare vacantly into space; the gentle ones who hide their faces and turn from all human contact; the restless ones who wander; whirl or rock aimlessly. ... There are some who speak endlessly but never communicate to anyone but themselves" (p.4). This was a perfect description of Kanner's infantile autism and, according to this pamphlet, these children were being placed in schools for mentally ill children. Over 20 years, no matter how much the definition of the diagnosis simmered, there had been no advancement or even attempt at a change in treatment.

The beginnings of change—1960s

Our pot that had been simmering with little change began to boil with controversy. *Time* magazine (1960) did a report on that the fact that Leo Kanner wrote an article on his life work for the *American Journal of Psychiatry*. The article in *Time* was very positive, applauding Kanner's contributions to child psychology. But at one point in the article, the writer for *Time* digresses briefly into the subject of Kanner's work with early infantile autism, and states that "all too often this child is the offspring of highly organized, professional parents, cold and rational—the type that Dr. Kanner describes as *just happening to defrost long enough to produce a child*" (p.78, my emphasis). In one short paragraph the reporter's words became Leo Kanner's words. The writer seemed to be quoting Kanner, but did Kanner really say this? Later, Kanner denounces this statement, but once the article is published it is too late. Into our boiling pot is placed the coined phrase "refrigerator type parent" (Rimland 1964, p.25). This added ingredient may have seemed slight, but it turned out to be very important. The specialists now began to think that they were tracking down the cause of this psychosis. It was after this article in *Time* that Dr. John Bowlby concluded that "maternal deprivation during infancy...is the cause of [this] schizophrenia as well as other major psychiatric disorders" (quoted in Milt 1963, p.13). Thus, in early 1960, the cause of infantile autism/childhood schizophrenia was now found, and blamed on the parents.

Also during this controversy, in 1962, a paper was written by psychologist Bernard Rimland for possible review in the Century Psychology Series. The paper titled "Infantile Autism, the Syndrome and its Implications for a Neural Theory of Behavior" received the Century Psychology Series Award for a work which "provided a significant contribution to the field of psychology". This paper, later published in book form in 1964, could be said to have been a stimulus for the psychiatric community to once again rethink the definition of this disorder. Rimland states emphatically that "the present writer's view is that there is sufficient information at hand to demonstrate clearly that early infantile autism is *not* the same disease or cluster of disease which has come to be called childhood schizophrenia, and that autism can and should be distinguished from it at all levels of discourse" (1964, p.68). After this eye opener, Rimland then looks at several theories on possible causes of autism. He is unable come up with any concrete conclusions for cause at this time, but at this point his lack of conclusions didn't matter. What mattered was that Rimland was one of the first to even suggest that there was a possible difference between infantile autism and childhood schizophrenia. Rimland's work seemed to bring the boiling pot of controversy overflowing with argument.

Controversy and positive changes—the early 1970s

Ten years later Michael Rutter of the Institute of Psychiatry in London wrote that "the diagnostic situation can only be described as chaotic. Clinicians from different centers use the same term to mean different conditions and different terms to mean the same condition" (Rutter 1972, p.315). His paper titled "Childhood Schizophrenia Reconsidered" was also read at the Taylor Manor Hospital Psychiatric Symposia Series on "Schizophrenia Around the World." In his opening statement, Rutter states: "We must conclude that the term childhood schizophrenia has outlived its usefulness. ... It is a disservice to child psychiatry to imply that today no differentiation is possible among the severe disorders of childhood" (p.315).

Rutter begins his argument by discussing what schizophrenia is. He points out that during the past eight years the World Health Organization (WHO) has studied long and hard to come up with a better "multi-axial approach to classification [of schizophrenia]" (p.318), and he notes that now that there is a different approach to classification, it is time to look differently at childhood schizophrenia. Rutter poses that "when schizophrenia presents as a psychosis in childhood it does so in a way which is basically comparable to that in adults. ... The diagnostic term schizophrenia is adequate and there is no need to add the adjective childhood any more than one might add the adjective adolescent, young adult or middle-aged" (p.321). In other words, according to Rutter, one is schizophrenic or not, not infantile, adolescent or adult. But if the child does not have childhood schizophrenia, then another term needs to be found. He argues that the term autism in the definition of schizophrenia means "a withdrawal into fantasy, but this is not what happens in the *syndrome* of autism. The schizophrenic may retreat from reality into fantasy, but the autistic child does not retreat, rather he *fails to develop* social relationships – a crucial distinction" (p.327, my emphasis).

After pointing out this important distinction, Rutter then compares schizophrenia to infantile autism. Step by step, he shows that there is a definite difference between the two—from age of onset to IQ levels (visual-spatial tasks, and language skills), from male to female ratio, to social class of parents and family histories (p.328). He states emphatically that "all these findings point to autism and schizophrenia being different disorders" (p.328). According to Rutter: "The evidence suggests that autism develops on the basis of a *central disorder of cognition* which involves the impairment of both the comprehension of language and defects in the utilization of language or conceptual skills in thinking" (p.329, my emphasis). He does not claim to know the cause of this cognitive defect, but he points out that in some cases it could be seen to be organic, developmental, or genetic (p.331). He admits that "in view of the very variable outcome and the very variable neurological findings ...biologically speaking the underlying pathology will probably prove to be quite heterogeneous [consisting of dissimilar parts]" (p.331). He too, like Rimland before him, did not find all of the answers, but he took the overflowing, boiling pot of controversy off the stove, placed it on the table, and the definition of autism was forever changed. The close connection with childhood schizophrenia was finally severed in that autism was no longer considered psychosis, but biological.

Furthermore, when Rutter addresses the controversial issue of cause, and the very controversial supposition that the parents of these children have a problem and are the cause of this disorder (refrigerator parents), he disputes it in one short paragraph by stating in part that "this issue has been reviewed previously with the conclusion that there is *no evidence* of any such abnormalities in family function or family relationships, as judged by studies using a variety of research techniques. Not all the possibilities have been systematically tested but the findings so far are negative" (p.331). He points out that there is a "consistent observation that the parents include a disproportionate number of professional and other middle class individuals" (p.331). But at this point he is unable to draw any further conclusions.

Hence this drastic change in definition caused a drastic change in treatment. During the next few years, there was "a rapid growth in the number of special schools and classes for autistic children" (Bartak and Rutter 1973, p.161). In their paper titled "Special Education Treatment of Autistic Children" Bartak and Rutter looked at three settings that were attempting to educate autistic children. They stated that their study "was designed to assess the value to autistic children of special education treatment and to evaluate the effects of different approaches to such treatment." One setting was a "psychotherapeutic unit with little emphasis on teaching," one setting "provided a structured and organized setting for the teaching of specific skills" and the last "used a more permissive classroom environment in which relationship and regressive techniques were combined with special educational methods" (pp.162–163). After studying information like time spent in free play compared to structured learning, the different curriculums, along with the progressive relationship of the teachers to the patients, unfortunately, the conclusion they came up with was not as definitive as they had expected.

Thus, due to the many variables involved, not only with the schools and treatment, but also with the individual children's conditions, they could only conclude that teaching these types of children was an art in itself and that "teachers involved in special education may adopt particular approaches to handicapped children which influence their educational process" (p.177). This information may seem like a very trivial thing for them to report, but actually, their study observed a major breakthrough. Up to this point, there had been very little "special education" of handicapped children going on. However, their report in 1973 documents the important beginnings of educational intervention for autism instead of the previous practice of institutionalizing these children.

Making it official—late 1970s through 1980s

By the late 1970s there was a mad scramble to prepare the other side dishes to bring to the table. Based on Rutter's work from 1978, the 1980 *Diagnostic and Statistical Manual* (DSM-III) of the American Psychiatric Association introduced the concept of Pervasive Development Disorder

(PDD) as the broad category in which autism was the "sole exemplar" (Cohen and Donnellan 1987). Along with this new definition were the following criteria of diagnosis: lack of attachment behavior; lack of or different eye-to-eye gaze; serious social difficulties with peers; difficulties in the pragmatics of speech; and lack of imaginative play (Rutter 1978, pp.139–152). Not only had Rutter succeeded in putting in place a new definition of autism, but he raised some interesting questions when he pointed out that "autism could turn out to be a behavioral syndrome without a *single* cause but nevertheless with a common *biological* causation, as is the case with cerebral palsy" (p.153). He adds that "it is far too early to regard the matter as settled" (p.153), but ends his paper on a positive note that "while we are still very far from a complete understanding of childhood autism, we are very much nearer that elusive goal" (p.156).

This DSM-III definition is what ushered in the 1980s, which can be summed up in one word—change. Not only was there a constant redefining of autism, but the treatment for autism evolved from "residential treatment" to "community" and from "segregated schools" to "classrooms in age-appropriate schools" (Frankel, Leary and Kilman 1987, p.337). Most importantly, the emphasis on education went from "behavioral traditional education for the mentally handicapped" to "social learning theory and functional curriculum" (p.333). As a result, the focus of the programs changed from "acquisition of preschool cognitive skills and behavior control" to "acquisition of *functional skills* and *socially appropriate* behavior needed to remain in the community" (p.337, my emphasis). These children were now not only being educated in regular schools, but also beginning to be taught how to function in the community.

Immediately after DSM-III appeared, a revision was undertaken. DMS-III-R was released in 1987 showing "diagnostic categories… changed from those in the DSM-III, but the classification as disorders of development and not as psychosis remained secure" (Wing 1997, p.148). In DSM-III-R, the name was finally changed from infantile autism to autistic disorder "to emphasize the condition throughout the life span" (Cohen and Volkmar 1997, p.17). Age of onset before the age of 30 months was dropped from the DMS-III-R criteria for autistic disorder due to the fact that it was felt that "the age of onset should not be considered a diagnostic feature…clinicians should rely on present examination rather than past history in making the diagnosis" (p.17).

Over the next few years, the definition for autistic disorder continued to be fine tuned, narrowed down and made more specific. Once again, almost immediately after the release of DSM-III-R, work began on a DSM-IV. The reason for the hurry was that the *International Classification of Diseases* (ICD-9) was drafting its tenth edition. These two systems, the DSM and ICD, were and still are the two main diagnostic systems in the field, and it was felt that there should be an agreement of what the DSM-III-R and the ICD-10 defined as autistic disorder (p.17).

Stabilization and agreement—1990s

In the early 1990s it was as if all of our side dishes were prepared and placed on the table along with the main meal. A sense of calm seemed to be felt as many of the key elements of definition, diagnosis and treatment were now in place. The definitions of autism according to the DMS-IV and ICD-10 agreed on the major issues that "old controversies over the supposed relationship between autism and schizophrenia, and over its postulated psychogenic causation, have disappeared as the evidence has made it clear that autism is a neurodevelopmental disorder, involving basic cognitive deficits, with genetic factors strongly predominant in etiology" (Rutter 1996, p.257). Not only was schizophrenia completely gone from the definition, but it was now understood that autism was not psychosis or mental illness, but neurological. An autistic child was now considered handicapped, just as a child with cerebral palsy, and this last major change is what had such a dramatic effect on treatment.

In fact, the 1990s may later be called the decade of the disabled child. What began as the Education for Handicapped Act (EHA) became the Individuals with Disabilities Act (IDEA). This act insured that autistic children (along with all handicapped children) have the right to "an appropriate education, at public expense, in the least restrictive environment" (Sullivan 1997, p.1012). Of course, none of these areas are free of controversy, even today. But once this law was in place, it then became the educator's job to assess the child and come up with a plan for that individual child's placement. At this time, the practice of "mainstreaming" was also introduced. In this approach the autistic child is no longer segregated, but placed into the regular classroom. The philosophy behind mainstreaming is that the child learns better among "normal" peers in the areas of social communication and social interaction. This term was then replaced in 1996 with the term "full inclusion." According to its supporters, the benefits are "increased expectations by teachers, behavioral modeling of normally developing peers, more learning, and greater self-esteem" (Mesibov and Shea 1996, p.337). The authors point out in their article that, in a sense, this is the ideal for autistic children. But because of the individual differences in this disorder, it is impossible to say that full inclusion will work with every autistic child (p.331).

It is because of these multiple differences among children with autistic disorder that the definition took one more step. In the late 1990s autistic disorder was redefined once again and is now defined as "autism spectrum disorders" (Lord 1997, p.460). The best way to explain this is if you imagine a rainbow as the spectrum, with the points of diagnosis blending into it. Each child's diagnosis can vary in severity from autistic-like, moderate autism, to classic severe autism, and within these divisions are differences in whether the child is verbal or non-verbal, differences in levels of IQ and skills, along with a wide variety of autistic behaviors. Most importantly, on this spectrum, there are no clear-cut lines as to where each child's diagnosis begins or ends. But if the child meets the DSM-IV criteria for autism, his or her diagnoses are somewhere along that spectrum. Not only does this spectrum help explain the diversity of each child, but it explains why a diagnosis of autism is so predictably unpredictable in its behaviors and symptoms.

Hence, in treatment, a plan is now created to handle this diversity, not only with autism, but with many other disorders. This plan is called an Individualized Education Program (IEP) and ideally is written for every child with a diagnosis of autism, no matter where that diagnosis falls on the spectrum. An IEP is written by a team of educators and the child's parents or guardians, and is the main ingredient in successfully educating a child with autism.

The most recent concerns—1998 to present

Now that our meal is served up, all of the dishes are placed, and everyone is around the same table, what is next for this disorder? In 1998 four researchers in the UK published a paper titled "Autism: The Phenotype in Relatives" (Bailey *et al.* 1998). It is interesting to note that in the beginning of their paper they too go back to Kanner: "Kanner [was among] the first to note parental personality characteristics that seemed to resemble the behavioral difficulties of the affected children" (p.369). They go on to say that once it was proven that autism was not *caused* by the way the parents raised a child as in Kanner's *supposed* "refrigerator parents" theory, it could be seen there was a definite "*biological* basis for autism" (p.369). The purpose of their paper was to "summarize knowledge about phenotypic expression in relatives and to outline some of the outstanding research questions" (p.370). After numerous pages of data, charts on parents and siblings, and various twin studies with family occurrence of autism, they conclude that "there are many unanswered questions about the phenotype in relatives of individuals with autism, but these now concern phenotypic definition and underlying mechanisms rather than *whether there is* a phenomenon to be explained" (p.388, my emphasis).

In other words, they now believe that there is a definite connection between these features or traits that "appear to have a genetic factor rather than environmental basis" (p.388) and it is their last statement that could be seen as a possible direction for the future study of autism. They state that "the particular skills of relatives, their preferred interests, and the characteristics of the partners they choose are all areas for future study that will provide a more complete picture of the phenotypic consequences of genes *predisposing* to autism" (p.389, my emphasis).

There are also studies being conducted which look at vaccinations and medications as a cause of autism. But at the moment there is no empirical evidence that either of these are the cause. Metabolic imbalances, chemical deficiencies, gastrointestinal disorders, viral or fungal infections and immune system disorders are also among the many areas that researchers are working in to figure out the cause of autism. None of these studies have any empirical evidence yet. But when we recall the past 60 years, look how far we have come and how much we have learned about this disorder.

Imagine again the little boy in preschool who was diagnosed as autistic. What a difference 60 years has made in his diagnosis and treatment. We have gone from thinking he has a mental illness—psychosis, brought on by "cold parents"—to realizing that for some, as yet, unexplained reason, his brain developed neurologically differently. Instead of taking this child and placing him in an institution for mental illness, he is being fully included in a regular classroom, and is being taught life skills to be able to function in society. In short, he is being treated as an individual, not as a diagnosis labeled autism.

When Leo Kanner wrote his "30-year" follow up on this disorder, he still wondered "what is it that explains all these [children's] differences?

Are there any conceivable clues for their eventual predictability?" (1971, p.145). The way to make an accurate prediction is by adding up the facts from the past. This is how the weather is predicted and how people trade on the stock exchange. Of course as a parent, it is what is happening now in the field of autism spectrum disorders that you need to be most concerned with. However, I believe that we also need to understand our past to be able to perhaps not predict but anticipate the future. Thus, after extensive reading I anticipate a positive future for my child. But please don't take my word for it. Do your own reading and trace your own history of autism. Because this history has now become part of your history, and what a fascinating history it is.

References

Bailey, A., Palferman, S., Heavey, L. and Le Coateur, A. (1998) "Autism: The Phenotype in Relatives." *Journal of Autism and Developmental Disorders 28,* 369–392.

Bartak, L. and Rutter, M. (1973) "Special Education Treatment of Autistic Children: A Comparative Study – 1. Design of Study and Characteristics of Units." *Journal of Child Psychology and Psychiatry 14,* 161–179.

Cohen, D.J. and Donnellan, A.M. (1987) "Preface." *Handbook of Autism and Pervasive Developmental Disorders.* New York: Wiley.

Cohen, D.J. and Volkmar, F.R. (eds) (1997) *Handbook of Autism and Pervasive Developmental Disorders,* 2nd edn. New York: Wiley.

Frankel, R.M., Leary, M. and Kilman, B. (1987) "Building Social Skills Through Pragmatic Analysis: Assessment and Treatment Implications for Children with Autism." In D.J. Cohen and A.M. Donnellan (eds.) *Handbook of Autism and Pervasive Developmental Disorders.* New York: Wiley.

Kanner, L. (1943) "Autistic Disturbances of Affective Contact." *Nervous Child 2,* 217–250.

Kanner, L. (1971) "Follow-up Study of Eleven Autistic Children Originally Reported in 1943." *Journal of Autism and Childhood Schizophrenia 1,* 119–145.

Lord, C. (1997) "Diagnostic Instruments in Autism Spectrum Disorders." In D.J. Cohen and F.R. Volkmar (eds) *Handbook of Autism and Pervasive Developmental Disorders,* 2nd edn. New York: Wiley.

Mesibov, G.B. and Shea, V. (1996) "Full Inclusion and Students with Autism." *Journal of Autism and Developmental Disorders 26,* 337–346.

Milt, H. (1963) *Serious Mental Illness in Children.* Public Affairs Pamphlet no. 352. New York: Public Affairs Committee.

Rimland, B. (1964) *Infantile Autism.* New York: Meredith.

Rutter, M. (1972) "Childhood Schizophrenia Reconsidered." *Journal of Autism and Childhood Schizophrenia 2*, 315–337.

Rutter, M. (1978) "Diagnosis and Definition of Childhood Autism." *Journal of Autism and Developmental Disorders 8*, 139–161.

Rutter, M. (1996) "Autism Research: Prospects and Priorities." *Journal of Autism and Developmental Disorders 26*, 257–275.

Sullivan, R.C. (1997) "Diagnosis Autism: You Can Handle It!" In D.J. Cohen and F.R. Volkmar (eds) *Handbook of Autism and Pervasive Developmental Disorders,* 2nd edn. New York: Wiley.

Time (1960) " The Child is the Father." July, 78.

Wing, L. (1997) "Syndromes of Autism and Atypical Development." In D.J. Cohen and F.R. Volkmar (eds) *Handbook of Autism and Pervasive Developmental Disorders.* 2nd edn. New York: Wiley.

chicken nugget #2

Challenges and failures

Treat people as if they were what they ought to be
and you help them to become what they are capable
of being.

(Johann Wolfgang von Goethe)

There is a difference between having unrealistic expectations for a child
and, as Goethe suggests, helping each child meet his or her potential. As
parents, it is up to us to find that fine balance with our own children. But
is there a rule of thumb that we can go by? Wouldn't it be nice if we had a
"potential-meter" that would allow us to feed information in about our
child along with information about the situation, and then it would spit
out a determination for us? *Yes, you should have your child attempt this*, or *No,
not right now.* Unfortunately there is no such tool, and I've found that the
best thing to do with my child is to go with my "gut" feeling. Call it
intuition, educated reasoning, or just plain common sense, every parent
can develop this ability. I call mine my "mom-meter." I use the
knowledge that I have learned about autism, match it with what I know
about my own child, and while he is attempting the activity, I watch for
signs telling me if he is enjoying the activity, or under too much stress.
Moments of stress are allowable, but we try to avoid outright misery.

When Jon was first diagnosed, we had no idea what his potential
would be. We literally took things one day at a time and progressed to
one week at a time. When he was seven years and all of the other kids his
age were signing up for summer sports, we put him in T-ball. I wrote an
introductory letter to the coach explaining a few things about my son
and autism. I included the facts that he may have to call my son's name a
few more times than others to get and keep his attention; my son's
reading level may be a year ahead of his peers, but his social skills were

almost two years behind; and that my child was the child likely to chase a butterfly all over the outfield and forget entirely that he was supposed to be participating in a game.

The coach was very supportive and assigned one of his "parent helpers" to coach Jon one on one in learning how to handle a ball. I sat on the bleachers during practices, and was so proud of the fact that he had a glove on his hand just like all of the other kids and was able to field a slow ground ball and toss it back to where it almost reached the coach. When he went up to bat, he was able to hit the ball off the T like the rest of the kids, but he needed someone running alongside him to get him to run towards the base or move to the next base. He didn't enjoy getting hot, or sweating, and he always sat down in the grass when he was in the outfield, but he basically had fun and seemed to enjoy the practices.

Then when it came to the games, I had a tough decision to make. Jon didn't understand the concept of a "game." He thought it was just "play" he was doing. I had to decide if I should leave him on the team and let him try to participate in competition or not. It's hard enough to get a neurotypical child to learn about competing and losing, but it is doubly hard for Jon, who still has to be greatly encouraged to try anything at all. Being a perfectionist and failing creates a huge amount of stress for him. If a task he is attempting doesn't "go right" he will "shut down," which usually means dropping to the ground in a lump or covering his face and crying. So, I used my mom-meter and made the decision to tell him that T-ball was over for the summer because the practices were over. We celebrated the last practice with drinks and snacks right along with the rest of the team, and I didn't explain to him that the team was going on to play real games against other teams every week. For Jon, at age seven, attending weekly practices, learning to catch and toss a ball and swinging a bat, along with trying to pay attention to verbal instructions in a group setting were enough challenges for him. Sometimes challenges have to be broken down into small steps, and this was how we broke this one down. Later, we could tackle competition, but for the moment, he had succeeded. Thus we learned early that challenge is good, learning to struggle is important. But there is a fine line between momentary stress and being miserable, and it was up to my husband and me to keep from crossing the line into misery.

Failure?

> There is no failure except in no longer trying.
>
> *(Elbert Hubbard, editor and publisher late 1800s)*

Everyone has a way of looking at life. Mine has always been rather optimistic. Along with Hubbard, I too believe that there really is no such thing as failure. Suppose you attempt something and it doesn't work out. You have learned something in the attempt. In every supposed failure, something is gained. Therefore, where is the failure?

When Jon turned ten, he became interested in the martial arts. I think he saw a "Doug" cartoon where Doug and his friends took karate lessons. So I called around and found a small studio that taught taekwondo. He attended the first "free" visitor session, where he stood out on the mat in shorts and t-shirt, working one on one with an instructor to learn a few basic moves. He was very excited at the end of the session and wanted to join. We purchased the white "uniform" right then and I signed him up. After I completed all of the paperwork, Jon went outside to wait for me, and I stood for a few minutes and gave the young man who had worked with him a "mini" introduction to Jon and autism. The young man seemed very excited and said that he'd heard that this type of structured training was good for people with disabilities. I too had read about a young autistic boy's success in the martial arts because of the structure and control involved in the art.

Thus, over the next few weeks we attended taekwondo twice a week. I sat behind a glass barrier and watched as the classes took place out on the mat. Instantly I was amazed at my son's level of concentration. From observing him I could tell that he was attentive and stayed engaged in the activity about 80 percent of the 90-minute session. For Jon and his autism, these were very high numbers. I was so proud as I watched him slowly work with the other instructor one on one and begin to learn and memorize the basic moves of the first routine. Yes, he had moments of frustration, but he was learning to work through them and, most importantly, he seemed to be enjoying himself.

About six weeks into the classes the instructors began splitting up the students, and every other class session, Jon would work with the owner of the studio, a woman, in a larger group setting. He seemed to adjust to this, but I could tell he was lagging a little bit behind as the other students moved across the floor and were all supposed to be in sync. He had a few difficult moments when they began their "mock" testing, preparing them for their first level of tests, but he seemed to be okay. When the real testing began, I noticed that Jon did best when he was teamed up with an older student and was able to "mirror" the other student's movements. After testing, he sat back down on the mat, and I gave him a thumbs up. He had half of the first routine down pat.

But at the next session, we found that Jon and a few of the younger students, ages six to eight, hadn't passed their first test. The owner of the studio turned the larger class over to the young man, and she took on Jon's smaller group that hadn't passed. I had, of course, spoken to her about Jon and autism, and I thought that she had understood his needs and potential delays. But during this session it became apparent that she did not. She lined up the five children in front of her and put Jon in front because he was the oldest. The male teacher had stood alongside Jon, allowing Jon to mirror his movements, while she stood facing them and clapped her hands, calling out the commands for each part of the routine. Jon was at a loss and looked around for someone to follow. After raising her voice to get my son's attention, loud enough that I could hear her through the glass, she told him to face forward and pay attention. As I watched the scene unfold, I felt my face grow warm, and I bit my lip to keep from jumping in.

This went on for most of the class session, and I could tell that Jon's stress level was rising. He had longer moments of inattention, and I could see him making wide-eyed expressions to himself in the mirror. The final blow came when the class was brought back together into the larger group. She had them quickly sidestepping in a circular motion, to learn balance and coordination, the inner circle going one direction, the outer circle, the other. I noticed that Jon's belt kept slipping loose. He would stop to tighten it, and the circle would have to stop, causing the others to bump into him and each other. I suppose if I hadn't been feeling my son's stress, and my mom-meter hadn't been going off the charts, I might have found it funny—all of the kids stopping and bumping into each other like dominos. But I suspect the teacher didn't find it funny either. She quickly stepped in and took Jon's belt away from him, tossing it up against the wall. Then she told them to continue.

When the circling was over and they lined up to be dismissed, Jon stood with his head bowed, holding his white jacket together. Yet, he seemed to be listening to her further instructions. Right before they began dismissing, the teacher retrieved Jon's belt, looped it over his shoulders and said something to him. Immediately I saw Jon fighting back tears. As they waited in line and were excused one at a time to be bowed off the mat, I watched as my son valiantly controlled his tears by blinking and swiping at his face. Of course my heart ached for him.

Later, when he came out of the locker room, he seemed fine and as we left I asked what the teacher had said to him when she gave him his belt back. He shook his head and said, "I don't know." I let the subject drop, and when I told my husband what had happened, he asked me if I had explained the situation to both teachers. Of course I had. This teacher just had a different way of teaching, and her methods didn't work well with Jon. My husband also questioned Jon about what had happened that day and wondered what the teacher said. Jon said, "Oh, never mind. Nothing." We couldn't get any more out of him.

The next few sessions Jon was back working with the male instructor, and the only thing I noticed was that he had more trouble paying attention than he had before. After these sessions, I asked him if he was still having fun and he said, "Yes," and then added, "But I won't ever pass." "Pass what?" I questioned. "Pass the test like the rest of the class." I assured him that he would, that he was doing a great job and had a lot of the first routine memorized. He sadly shook his head.

Within the next week I noticed that his sadness was increasing. This time, on the way to class, I noticed that he was sunk down in the seat beside me. "What's wrong?" I asked. "I have a headache," he said. This from a child who rarely complains of any aches or pains. I told him that he would be fine and maybe he was just hungry. We drove through a fast food restaurant and parked outside the studio, eating in the car. I tried to talk to him, to see what was going on, telling him again that he was doing fine and I was very proud of him. But I couldn't get much of a response from him. When he finished eating, he once again slumped down in the seat. I asked him again if he was still having fun. "I don't know," was his answer. I sat for a few minutes in silence, as my gut instinct tried to tell me something. "I have an idea," I said. "What?" came his not too interested reply. "Why don't we drive over to the college and see if we can get you into those swim lessons that we heard about?" It was like a light went off inside the car. He sat straight up. "Really?" he asked. "Yes," I said. But went on to explain that he couldn't do both taekwondo and swimming. "Okay! Swimming!" he exclaimed.

We backed out of the parking lot as the female owner pulled in. She would be the instructor for that night's class. As we passed her, my son waved at her in glee. On the way to the college I made sure that he knew that these were 14 days of lessons and that he had to finish them. He asked several questions, and when it seemed like I had satisfied him with enough answers, he suddenly picked up the taekwondo uniform, dropped it over the back seat, and said "Whew! Great idea, Mom!"

Was taekwondo a failure? I don't think so. Jon attended twice a week for ten weeks. He paid attention more than he had in any other sport, and he gave it his best shot. When the stress level of testing and the teacher's method of teaching got to be too much for him, I had to decide if it was time to push him to continue, or perhaps move on. I went with my instincts and we moved on. He joined the swim classes, completed the first session, and has since taken two more 14-day sessions.

Would I do it all over again? Would I put him back into another martial arts class, or let him attempt another group "sport?" Yes. We don't know what Jon's potential is unless we challenge him to attempt things. The failure is not making the attempt. But for right now, I will continue using my mom-meter, until one day he develops his own meter. Then I will have to sit back and let him monitor himself. He can do it. I have an optimistic outlook.

Additional thoughts

Should I have taken the female instructor aside and again explained my son's needs to her—suggesting better ways that she could work with him? Perhaps. But at the time I was very angry, and only wanted to give her a piece of my mind. Later, after I had calmed down, I decided that if I gave everyone who misunderstands my child a piece of my mind, I might not have any mind left. You have to pick your battles, and in this case, I chose not to fight this battle. If I had it to do over again, maybe I would do it differently. Maybe I did make a mistake.

In addition, a very interesting thing happened recently when I was finishing up this book. One day when I was at the local university for early registration, a young man stopped me and asked if I remembered him. When I only stared at him, he explained that he had been my son's taekwondo instructor. "Ah yes," I said, shaking his hand and at the same time remembering this chapter from my book.

He gave me an apologetic smile, and said that he had been wanting to get in touch with me and my son since "that day" when we had quit coming. He explained that he had given the owner his notice that day, due in part to what had happened with my son. I was at a complete loss for words as he added that he had wanted to find us to apologize, and tell us that he no longer worked for her.

Finally when I found my voice, I accepted his apology of course, and told him that I realized then that he'd had no control over the situation. Then I told him about this chapter in my book on my son's taekwondo experience. He cringed when I mentioned that the title of the section was "Challenges and failures" and I quickly explained to him that the point was that I did not consider my son's experience at taekwondo a failure, but a success, because both he and I had learned a lot from having gone through it. This brought another apology from him, which I again told him was not needed. He said he was glad that he had seen me again, and I wished him luck in his studies as he walked away.

I remember standing and watching him for a few minutes and wondering what were the chances of running in to him, or that he would recognize me after all these years? Another success to make note of, but I don't know who was responsible for this one.

Chapter Three
Asking the right questions

It is better to know some of the questions than all of the answers.

(James Thurber)

This is the age of the internet. If a parent sits down at the computer, connects to the World Wide Web and types in the word "autism," the good news is that there is a lot more information out there. The bad news is that there is a lot more information out there! Where does a parent begin? How do we keep up with it all, and how do we sift the good from the bad?

Years ago, when my son was diagnosed, I thought the most practical place to start was the local library. I admit we do live in a small town, but when I typed in "autism" on the card catalog, only one book came up. I'm afraid I don't remember the title, or the author, but I do remember that the publication date was 1973. The director of special services at the school had told me that because the definition of autism had changed so drastically, to stay away from any information published before 1990. Thus, in my first search, I came up empty handed. Where did I go from there? I went to the "big city" and stood in the aisle of a bookstore, unashamedly reading through books that I couldn't afford to purchase. After all, this was my child we were talking about. I was determined to get information one way or another.

Fortunately, parents nowadays have more access to information, not only because of the internet, but because of the flood of information being written about autism. At that time there were very few books like the one you are holding, handwritten by a parent who is trying to share information to help someone else get through this diagnosis. But, today, you can find in the local bookstores a complete section of books written by parents, not only on autism but on many other disabilities. Unfortunately, this wealth of information can sometimes be counterproductive, in that it overwhelms us. Yes, there is more information, but the question still remains the same: where does a parent start?

I believe one of the best places to start is being able to ask the right questions. Slightly off the topic of autism, I will never forget my mother-in-law's first experience with doctors in the United States. She is from a different country and had been raised in an environment where doctors were pretty close to gods, and one never questioned anything a doctor said. At that time, because of her lack of English, I went with her to translate. The doctor was suggesting a minor surgery, but I asked all of the right questions, and we discovered that perhaps she didn't have to have this surgery if she could adjust her medication. A month later, after doing just that, she wasn't having any more problems, and surgery wasn't needed. I remember my mother-in-law bragging to my husband how I had stood up to the doctors and kept asking questions. She thought it was an amazing feat, when in fact, I was doing only what came naturally to me. Culturally, my mother-in-law hadn't been taught to ask questions, while I had.

But how do we ask questions concerning a subject we know very little about? At the time of my son's diagnosis, a chapter like this would have been a goldmine to me, because before I could find the answers to my child's situation I needed to know what to ask. Hence, following is a list of ideal questions to initially ask. I've tried to group them in a logical, progressive order, but feel free to skip to the point that is relevant to what you are going through at this time. When it comes to answers, I may be providing you with a few, to help you further your research, but unfortunately I can't provide you with all of the answers. Remember, my child's diagnosis, and life, are going to be different from your child's diagnosis. These are the right questions, but we each have to find the right answers for our own children.

Where do I start?

What is autism?

You will find the most current answer to this in the *Diagnostic Statistical Manual for Mental Disorders: DSM-IV-TR* (APA 2000). This is the Bible when it comes to official information on autism. What it will tell you is that "autism" is the most widely used term in a range of disabilities that this source refers to as pervasive developmental disorders. Autism is a neurological developmental disability that affects the way people understand and relate to what they see, hear and sense. Autism results in problems of levels of severity in social relationships, communication differences, and behavior. You will, of course, find similar definitions on the internet, and in every book you pick up. But make sure that the other definitions you find are in agreement with the DSM-IV-TR, because this source is the one that is always updated and current on any information involving autism.

How do you know my child is autistic?

The characteristics of autism will be in four to five areas of development, but will differ with each individual in severity:

- delays in verbal language development

- delays in understanding social relationships

- inconsistent patterns in sensory responses

- uneven patterns of intellectual functioning

- marked restriction of activity and interests.

As you read other books and material, you may find these areas defined differently or the wording changed, but they should still fall into the following areas: physical, social and language skills; abnormal responses to sensations; problems with speech, language and non-verbal communication; and abnormal ways of relating to people, objects, and events.

What caused my child's autism?

At the present time, the cause of autism is still unknown. Here is where you will find an onslaught of information. Scientists believe they are getting closer to finding the answer. It may be caused by genetics, as Down syndrome, or it is a possible combination of several things, or something that is a "trigger" for autism that they are as yet unaware of. They do know that it is not caused by the psychological environment of the child, meaning that the theory that a non-nurturing parent causes autism is not true. I suggest researching this question carefully, and once again, referring to the DSM-IV-TR.

Is there a cure for autism?

As yet, there is no known cure for autism. You may find information out there that states otherwise, and I do realize that when a parent states that their child has been cured, usually they mean that their child's previous symptoms of autism spectrum behaviors are gone. But remember to read carefully.

Can my child be helped?

Yes. Most definitely. Autism is treatable. There is almost too much information out there on this subject, and because this information is so crucial, it must not only be sifted through carefully, but individualized to meet your child's needs.

Will my child lead a normal life?

Normal, no. Nearly normal? It depends on the individual, the diagnosis, the behaviors. Each child is different in the severity of disability. Many times I have heard the statement: "The most predictable thing about autism is that it will be *un*predictable." What affects one child may not have any effect on another. What one child may have a problem with, another child doesn't. Autism is an *individual* disability that cannot be predicted from one child to the next.

After a basic understanding of autism, what do I do now?

How can I help my child?

Special therapies, education, treatments, they are all out there, and this is where you must educate yourself, and qualify everything with your child's needs. The point to remember is, don't take a back seat in planning your child's program: you are the driver. When the school sends a conference notice home for you to sign, make sure you read it, sign it, and attend. If you can't attend at the time they give you, get on the phone and reschedule a time that works for you. You live with your child 24 hours a day. The people that are helping are experts in their field: you are the expert on your child. What better team is there to help your child than you teamed up with them?

What do I do if I disagree with the educators, administrators, or experts?

Tell them. Speak up if not for yourself, for your child. Disagree. Question. Make them explain it to you again until you come if not to an agreement then an understanding, and a possible way to work things out. When they give you the handout titled "Procedural Safeguards for Children and Parents" (or whatever handout your state requires), read it. Know your rights as a parent of a child with a disability.

What is an IEP?

This stands for Individual Education Plan (some states refer to this plan differently). This plan is basically a map for your child's future. It is a joint document put together by you and the team members. It contains the following: current level of performance, annual and long-term goals, short-term objectives, and services that are needed for your child.

The IEP team should include one or both parents, or guardians, the child's teachers, any aides, special class teachers (such as music, PE), school administrators, any staff that may be working with your child (such as bus drivers), and perhaps a parent advocate or your attorney if need be. By law, the IEP team must meet at least once a year, but the parents or other members may request a meeting at any time. (In the early days, when there is a major transition going on in my son's life, we meet every two weeks.)

Something I didn't know until I was told later is that the IEP should not already be written and brought to the meeting, but put together at the meeting with your input. Most importantly, you do not have to sign this document at the meeting. Tell the members that you wish to take a copy home with you to be able to read it over and consider it. In addition, just recently I was told by a parent that because they had signed the "attendance" form, a form passed around at the beginning of a meeting to record who was there, this was later construed that they were already in agreement with the IEP that the educators had brought to the meeting, even though they hadn't signed the IEP itself. Don't be paranoid, but be cautious in what you sign.

After years, I am still learning about IEPs and what they should include. As my child's life changes, his IEP will evolve also. You will find several examples on the internet of IEPs that will help you to write your own child's map.

After the IEP is written and signed, what if one part of it is not working for my child?

Ask about it. Yes, you signed the IEP, but that doesn't mean it is set in stone. Call the case manager, the person who is in charge of your son's meetings, and discuss your concerns with her. If she doesn't call a special meeting to address the issues, you call the meeting.

After a diagnosis, and after an IEP, now what do I do?

Will my child be in a "regular" classroom? If not, where will he/she be?

After the IEP is signed, then it needs to be implemented. One of the first steps is deciding what type of classroom your child will be placed in. If he/she will be "mainstreamed" into a regular classroom, will there also be a one-on-one aide assigned to your child? What will that aide's responsibilities and goals be? If your child will not have an aide, how will the teacher be able to meet any special needs your child may have, along with teaching the other 20 to 28 students in the classroom? If the best placement for your child is into a smaller "special services" classroom, how many teachers will be working with how many students? Will your child be learning the regular grade curriculum that his/her other peers are learning in the classroom? How many hours a day will he/she be in this classroom, and with his/her peers? (For example, when will he/she be attending music class, PE, or art?)

As you can see, once your child is placed in the "best educational setting" you will still need to ask the right questions, and to make sure that you understand exactly what is being done for your child. What if the environment that he/she is placed in doesn't seem to be working after a while? Most educators will suggest giving it more time, which of course is good common sense. But in the end, if it's not working, it's not working. Remember you can call an IEP meeting and change his/her educational plan. The most important thing is to find what works best for your child, no matter how much trial and error it takes.

What type of "pull-out" services will my child be receiving, i.e., speech, occupational therapy, or physical therapy or any others?

Remember treatment varies with every child, but most children with a diagnosis of an autism spectrum disorder will be receiving some speech (language) therapy, occupational therapy, physical therapy, or other services. The important thing to know is that these services are provided by the school district as part of your child's education. Other possible services provided by the state, according to the state you live in, could be: respite care, before and after school care, summer programs, recreational programs, group homes and residential living programs. There are many state agencies that can help you. The best thing is to get on your state's website for disabilities.

When my son was diagnosed, we couldn't have been in a better school district. They sent his future teacher and an aide to a special training seminar on autism. (He was the first in their school diagnosed as high functioning autistic and would be the first to be in the regular classroom.) In addition, throughout the years, he has been pulled out a designated number of hours for speech and occupational therapy, and, up to sixth grade, he has had a one-on-one classroom aide. But unfortunately getting services for a child with a diagnosis of an autism spectrum disorder varies greatly, not only from state to state but from school district to school district.

When my son was entering the third grade, we moved from one school district to another and I was more than a little worried about what I would find. We were going into a much larger school system, and I had spoken to a few parents who'd had problems with special services. As soon as we discovered that our new home would be in the other school district, I asked our present director of special services to please contact the other district and set up a meeting to begin the transition.

At this first meeting were my husband and I, the new district's director of special services and their "autism specialists." I carried with me my son's school records and previous IEP, and I remember telling them point-blank that I was very concerned about moving into their district because of the size difference. They were immediately full of reassurances, and my husband and I sat and listened to their plans for transition, which involved: planning who my son's teacher would be before the school year was over, so she could visit him in his present classroom; sending his future aide to a class on autism; holding an in-service on autism for all of the other teachers (music, PE, art), and letting him visit his new school as soon as possible. By the end of the meeting I felt much better and less stressed, and I told them it sounded like things were going to work out. But I also told them that they needed to know one thing about my husband and me. We take an active role in our son's education, and because the school district was so large, we were determined to see to it that our son would not become just a case file or another number. I remember the director sitting with her mouth open at this comment, not quite knowing what to say. Yes, harsh words from a parent whose child hasn't even been in their school district yet, but I do not regret taking a strong stand from the very beginning. Of course, we have had our ups and downs, but my husband and I have continued to be in the driver's seat, which is where we belong.

After I have a diagnosis, placement and services: what next?

What is the prognosis for my child, or what will the future bring?

The answer to this question varies just as it does with "normal" developing children. Some people with autism go on to higher education, or can work certain jobs. Some autistics live as independently as possible. Of course, it comes down to where your child is on the autism spectrum. These days, it is much easier for a person with a disability to find their niche in the community compared to even five years ago; easier, but not easy.

As your child moves through the school system, you will still need to stay on top of things. When your child is in the teen years, you should start looking at transition services into the community. Most school systems offer "life skills" classes in managing finances, cooking, and other basic independent living skills. The best school systems also offer job coaching, job shadowing and job placement for young adults with special needs. It is your young person's right to get these services, and don't let a school system tell you otherwise.

Will my autistic child grow up and be able to get married and have children?

Another question that, of course, differs from individual to individual. Some high functioning adults do go on to have relationships, date and possibly marry. There are several organizations on the internet and in a few communities which are set up only for adults with an autism spectrum disorder. I see this as a real breakthrough that shows how people with this disability are returning from the margins of society to become more a part of it. However, just as you can't predict the future for any "normal" child, you can't predict it for your autistic child either.

What you can do is keep at it. Keep asking those questions. Realize that your child's learning and education do not stop when he or she is 18 or 19, and that your help for them can't stop at that time, either. Is helping your child a lifetime job? Yes. Will it always be a miserable, difficult, road to drive? No. Will you ever be able to stop the questions? I don't think so, because I have one more important question for you. If you don't keep asking the questions for your child, who will?

Questions I have asked over the years, which may help you also

1. Where does my son's diagnosis lie on the autism spectrum?

2. What is the difference between high functioning autism and Asperger's Syndrome, and how would changing his official diagnosis affect his IEP?

3. Is a full-time, one-on-one aide the best thing for my child?

4. What do we do about his finicky eating habits?

5. Why can't he have a computer available to him in the classroom if this helps him to get his work done?

6. Why shouldn't each one of his teachers attend his IEP meeting, from classroom teacher to PE?

7. How do I find the fine line between helping my child to make friends and forcing peer relationships on him that he has no interest in having?

8. What does my child want to be when he grows up, and how can I help him to achieve this goal, taking into consideration his special needs?

9. When and how do I try to explain to my child that he has something called autism?

10. Do boys with autism develop physically during adolescence at the same rate as other boys?

11. If my child continues to have success in the regular classroom, do I strike the diagnosis of high functioning autism from his school records, so that he no longer has a label following him around?

12. How will a decision that I must make for my child affect his happiness?

13. Do my husband and I apply for continued guardianship after the legal age limit?

As you can see, every one of us has our work cut out. Your questions will be different from my questions because they will be about your child. Just please remember, don't quit asking.

References and more great sources for great questions

American Psychiatric Association (APA) (2000) *Diagnostic and Statistical Manual for Mental Disorders: DSM-IV-TR.* Washington, DC: APA.

Center for the Study of Autism: "Frequently Asked Questions about Autism." www.autism.com

Grandin, T. (Dr. Grandin is high functioning autistic) www.autism.org/temple/faq.html

National Autism Society – Frequently Asked Questions Menu. www.oneworld.org/autism_uk/fazs/faq.html

TEACCH – Autism primer: "Twenty Questions and Answers" www.teacch.com/20ques.htm

chicken nugget #3

The "After-the-IEP-Meeting Chant"

> In this world nothing is certain but death and taxes.
>
> *(Benjamin Franklin)*

And for some of us, IEP meetings. For those of you who are just getting started with your child's education, this nugget may worry you, but to be forewarned is forearmed. IEP meetings are no fun. Hmmmm—not really strong enough. IEP meetings can be a parent's worst nightmare. Yes, much better. IEP meetings go on the same list as appearing in traffic court and having to plead guilty, getting a root canal, and delivering a baby without medication. All three are events that some of us have gone through, usually because we had no choice in the matter, and all four events are upsetting, depressing and, at times, physically painful. IEP meetings are something that a parent who has a "normal" child cannot relate to, and something that a parent of a child with a disability wishes that they didn't relate to so well. But enough of this ranting, let me give you a possible explanation for IEP misery.

It was at an IEP meeting, your first, that you were told that your child has a disability. Some educators handle this first meeting very well, others, unfortunately, not so well. But no matter how sensitive they try to be, they are telling you that there is something wrong with your child. You may have had some concerns about your child before the meeting, but this is *the* meeting. This is where, after a lot of testing, and possible visits to medical experts, they have put the diagnosis in writing. This is where they begin to map out a plan for your child to enable him to get through the school system, and, later on, into the community. These people really do have your child's best interests in mind, even if it does always feel like an us vs. them battle. But because of this first IEP meeting, where you are told what the "label" is that they are putting on your child, you will never be able to have positive feelings about these meetings.

Even later on, when you've had several meetings under your belt, they may still depress you. Why is that? I believe one reason is that you are going along, taking things one day at a time—getting your child to school, helping with homework, helping with daily living skills, helping on outings, at out-of-school activities—in other words, you have found a fairly comfortable routine. Then the scheduled IEP meeting rolls around and—blam! You go into the meeting and are reminded of a stark reality: your child has a disability. Yes, your child is a "happy camper" most of the time. This is because of the routine that you, and everyone else, has helped to establish. But for an hour or more you sit and talk about your child's disability. You talk about what is not working and how it can be changed. You talk about the fact that your child is not meeting certain goals, and so these need to be readdressed. During this hour, you forget your happy child, and are forced to focus on your disabled child. Depressing, oh, how depressing. But necessary? Yes. Now you see the root canal connection? Something that hurts terribly, you absolutely hate it, but, oh, how necessary.

So, what is a parent to do if IEPs are a necessary evil? How do we cope with them? One way that I have already mentioned is to try to be positive. Yes, you must discuss your child's problems and failings during this meeting, but why not end on a positive note? If you don't point out your child's strengths and skills, possibly no one else at the meeting will. I always try to end on the positive, and my son's team members have now gotten so used to this that at times they bring up the positive themselves.

Another way to handle this necessary evil is by keeping a sense of humor, even though it may not be funny at the time. The Mothers From Hell 2 organization that I belong to has printed buttons that read "Who's IEP is it, anyway?" I've always been tempted to wear my button into a meeting, but haven't gotten up the nerve yet. But when they are talking about trying to teach your child "spontaneous" social interactions, try to see the humor that if it's "spontaneous" it can't be taught, can it? I must admit that I can't see the humor sometimes until after the meetings, but then I try to find at least one chuckle.

My husband and I also try to make these meetings less stressful by always sticking to a strategy that we call "good cop, bad cop" (just like on

Miami Vice). Yes, our school district has been very supportive, but we don't know if it is because of our persistence or whether all families get this support. Therefore, when we go into a meeting, I'm the "bad cop" and my husband is the "good cop." I come to every meeting with a list of things that I want to talk about—a list of questions. I present my issues, ask my questions, sometimes get things stirred up a little (even with a supportive team it's inevitable), and my husband then calms everyone down, sometimes with a joke. Over the years, we have found that this strategy works well for us.

But once when I was very tired and overly stressed about an issue, I told my husband we had to switch roles, and that it was his turn to demand, and I would calm things down. I was tired of being the "baddie." He agreed, and we went into the meeting. Unfortunately, halfway through the meeting, when the important issue finally came up, I could sit quietly no longer. I jumped right in, laying out on the table exactly what we were asking, and why. My husband even passed me his notes, where he had the "right" questions written down. He then followed up my statements with his typical softening act. Later on, we laughed about it, and I realized that no matter if I liked the job or not, I was the "bad cop." I just can't sit and keep my mouth shut while an educator says something I totally disagree with. We've never switched roles again.

But in the end, if being positive, remembering a sense of humor and having a strategy still do not put an end to after-the-IEP depression, there is always the "After-the-IEP-Meeting Chant." To be effective, this chant should be said not only after the meeting but before, and sometimes, you may need to whisper it to yourself during the meeting. It goes like this:

> I'm okay. My child will be okay. The meeting went okay. Life will go on. I can get through another one of these meetings for my child's sake. It could be worse. I can't think of a worse scenario at the moment, but I'm sure there is one out there…I'm okay…it's all okay… It could be worse.

You get the picture. Feel free to write your own.

Chapter Four

A day in the life of autism

To be silent is not to be mute, it is refusing to speak, and so, to speak still.

(Jean-Paul Sartre)

Imagine if you could, going for five hours without speaking. Or perhaps you don't go without speaking, but for five hours you go without carrying on a real conversation with anyone. When you speak, your words are to yourself—into the air—perhaps in a sing-song. Finally, if you do speak to another person, it is very brief, only asking or answering a question.

Each of the above scenarios took place one semester when I was able to observe three children who have diagnoses of autism. The first silence, not saying a word for approximately five hours, was my own silence, because I didn't want to interfere with any of the children while I was observing them. The other two scenarios of silence, talking to themselves, speaking only to ask or answer a question, took place during each visit, with each child. What amazed me about these children's silences was that all three seemed to be very happy, content children within their silence. Although they were all placed in a regular classroom setting (mainstreaming), they were still in an autistic silence the majority of the time. Sartre probably didn't plan to describe the world of autism when he wrote his theory of silence in *What is Literature?*, but he describes the autistic world perfectly: silent, not mute—but refusing to speak, and so speaking still. This is the world of autism, a speaking silence.

I tried to enter this world by doing what writer Mary Sue MacNealy (1999) describes as a "casual ethnographic research." MacNealy states that with this type of research "a researcher interested in a certain community or environment might visit there to get an overall first impression from an outsider's perspective" (p.217). So, although I was a parent of one of the children, I aimed for an "observational distance" from all three. After doing these observations, the researcher's job is to then write a casual report about what occurred, not trying to draw major conclusions, or cite great statistics, but simply a report of their findings. Thus, the researcher gets an impression of the community and may decide to do further in-depth research.

I read the word "community" in this definition, and decided that I wanted to observe a day in the autism community. During the past several years, I have begun to think differently about autism, deciding that it really is more a *place* than a diagnosis. To me, it is as if my child lives in two worlds, the *now* and the *autistic*, and I admit that it fascinates me how easily he can travel between the two. Thus, I chose to do a casual ethnographic observation of not only my own child but two others with a diagnosis of autism spectrum disorder, with the goal of perhaps gaining more understanding of the *community* of autism. What you will find in this chapter is information about how I did the observations and several interesting things that I learned. Please remember that these are my observations, as a parent of one of these children. Although I tried to be as impartial an observer as possible, I still couldn't help but bring my own thoughts and feelings to this observation. But the main thing I came away with was the strong belief that every parent should try to do a day-long observation, not only of their own child but other similar children if possible. I believe if you do this, your entire perspective will be drastically, and irrevocably, changed.

Preliminaries

To gain access to observe any community, one needs all types of permission forms. To observe my own child, I had to gain the principal's permission as well as his teacher's. For the other two students, both parents gave me written permission to observe their children and write up any information that I gained from my observations. A copy of this permission form then went to each student's principal and teacher. When writing about these children, I will refer to each by their grade levels, fourth grader, fifth grader and seventh grader, but this is not to demean the importance of these children in any way. Yes, I watched them as an ethnographic researcher, but at no time during the day did they become mere "case studies" to me. I only refer to them in this way to protect them and their families' privacy. I also asked each parent to keep a morning and, if possible, evening journal, describing in detail the home life before school and after school, so that I could hopefully gain a sense of what their entire day was like.

During the time that I was observing, I kept quiet and tried to be as inconspicuous as possible, thus keeping my interaction with each child to a minimum. Each class was told by its teacher that I was there to visit and observe the class, and to learn how classroom aides worked in the classroom. Since all three of these students have one-on-one teacher's aides to help them, this reason was given to explain why I left the room every time the child and his aide left the room. Overall, these three days of observations were very successful.

I was at each student's school when they arrived first thing in the morning, and was able to go comfortably everywhere with them. I was able to take extensive notes on each child, on the left side of the page writing the child's behaviors, interactions, any conversations or distractions, and on the right side I made my personal comments, listed a question, or my own opinion. During the times when it was more beneficial for me to sit without writing and just watch, I did so, and wrote the notes as soon as possible within the next hour.

Since this was an informal observation, an obvious question would be, did I learn anything? My answer would have to be that I learned too much, and that I will still be learning from this experience probably for months to come. What I found difficult when I sat down to write was trying to decide what to put in and what to leave out. I realized that it wouldn't be practical for me to give a detailed moment-by-moment description of each child's day, and so decided the best way to organize my observations was by talking about similarities and differences. But even then I found that I had to narrow down the observations to only a few categories. Of course, in discussing similarities and differences, I do realize that not only are these three children different and unique as human beings, but that they are all three different in their diagnoses along the autism spectrum. To me, these differences only added more worth to my study. For it is really their differences that make them who they are and served as a wake up call that said: Hey, there's a unique kid in there!

Beginning the day in autism

By reading over the parents' morning journals, I noticed that both the fourth grader and seventh grader woke up by themselves in the mornings and were watching TV by 6:00 a.m. The fifth grader, however, had to be physically woken up, and encouraged to take a quick morning shower. The fourth grader and fifth grader both had breakfast at home and were driven to school by a parent. The seventh grader waited for the regular school bus and ate his breakfast in the cafeteria after arriving at school.

Once each student arrived, all three sat without talking to anyone else, and waited for the bell to ring. The fifth grader waited silently in a huge, crowded gymnasium, the seventh grader ate his breakfast, in silence, in a bustling cafeteria, and the fourth grader silently watched about 15 minutes of a Disney movie along with about 40 other children. All three were surrounded by a lot of children during this time, who of course were not silent. Yet none of their peers approached any of the children at this time and said hello, or tried to chat with them as they were doing with all of the other students.

The school day started at 8:30, and when I looked back over the first few hours I saw that during the first two and a half hours, the interaction for each child had only been with a parent telling them to eat their breakfast or get themselves dressed for school. The fourth grader did question his mom about taping his show for him while he was at school, and the fifth grader's first question of the morning was if he could rent a certain video. It seemed that there was not much being in the now yet for these children.

To aide or not to aide?

As I noted, all three children had aides who worked closely with them throughout the day. The fourth grader's aide sat immediately next to him so that the aide could whisper instructions throughout the day. The fifth grader's aide was at a further distance, yet close to the child in the back of the room, and stood in the general vicinity to see if he needed any help. The seventh grader's aide also sat at a desk next to the student—within whispering distance. Thus, each aide worked differently with each child.

The fourth grader's aide helped with instructions and reminded the child to focus. At one point, I noticed that when the children were in the library and given an assignment to do, the aide physically filled out the work sheet for the child while trying to get him to stay focused and look up the information in the reference books that they were using. But from where I was sitting I could tell that the child was definitely not interested and was "out" more than "in," resulting in the work getting completed, but in the aide's handwriting. During the day, there were also several times when the aide helped his student interact with other classmates. At these times, the aide almost seemed like another peer, and acted as a buffer or bridge from his student to the other students by getting them involved in a conversation with each other, no matter how stilted or mechanical.

The fifth grader's aide was more like an additional teacher in that she was there to answer questions and ask the student questions, but she did not work with the student as closely as the fourth grade aide did. For almost a total of five hours this student did not once speak to a classmate while in the classroom, in line, or doing work. He raised his hand to ask questions of the teacher, he motioned to the aide to ask questions and he answered both adults when he was questioned. It wasn't until he was in the library, without the aide, that he turned to one of his classmates to help him. He interacted more in those 30 minutes in the library with his peers than he had during the five hours up to that point.

The seventh grade aide worked more constantly with the student, helped him to stay focused, asked questions, and even during a break played computer games with him. This student had been in the regular classroom up until that month, but for some reason he was no longer able to stay up with the academics in the regular seventh grade classes, or keep up with the other students. The school had recently decided to place this student, along with his aide, into a small special services classroom where the aide was able to work closer with him on each assignment and there would be less distractions or pressure from being in the regular classroom. Thus, I watched as the student worked each lesson with the aide close by, went to another room for "consumer math," where they played "store" to learn how to buy things and count change, and after lunch, the aide played computer games with the student as a reward for getting his morning work done. This student also did not interact with any peers at all throughout the day and it was as if the aide was not only his teacher, but his peer.

In and out…in and out…in and out

Throughout the day, it became easier to tell when the students were in their autistic world and when they were in the present, or the now. Much of my notetaking ended up becoming coded so that I could see the shift from their world to ours. What totally amazed me about this shifting back and forth was that all three students did it constantly, and that the fourth and fifth graders were able to follow the teachers' directions even when they were *in* autism. More than once when I was watching these two students, I could tell that they were *in* a video or story in their head. At times, they were even talking or laughing to themselves. However, if the teacher was giving the class directions during this *in* autism time, both students were able to immediately follow through with the directions and didn't seem to miss a beat.

The seventh grader had more difficulty staying focused, but I did notice that even during his *in* autism time, he was very aware of what was happening around him. The classroom that he had been placed in was for behavior disorder (BD) students. At certain times throughout the day, the other teacher raised his voice at a student, or one of the other students caused a disturbance. Although the student that I was observing sat with his back to all the other kids, I could tell that he was eying what was going on over his shoulder. Even when he was obviously in autism, his gaze stayed on the scene unfolding behind him, and at one point, an argument out in the hallway. When the aide crossed the room towards him, intending to tell him to get back on task, he immediately noticed her movements, and he came back to the now, trying to get himself on task.

Rewards = their interests

Obviously, each one of these children was at a different place on the autism spectrum and throughout the day each child displayed his own special skills or interests. In fact, the best part of the day was when each child was allowed free time, usually as a reward for getting some of their work done. The fourth grader fascinated me with his interest in drawing. He would take page after page and draw his favorite cartoon characters depicted in different scenes. After watching him do this a few times, I realized that he was copying the scene out of the book that he was flipping through or from the computer in front of him. Hence, his favorite character, similar to Charles Shultz's Lucy character, was drawn into a fairy-tale forest from the book he was reading or into a Garfield comic strip because he was looking at Garfield on a computer program. Each one of these scenes were drawn with a "quick sketch" technique and finished, full of detail, within seconds. I also noticed in his parents' journal from the morning and evening that he spent a lot of time on the internet, drawing scenes, incorporating what he saw.

The fifth grader's reward during the day was that when he finished his work he could read his library book. This student had just discovered fiction books in fifth grade and was reading his way through a mystery series about Hank the Cow Dog—all 50 titles. Each time that he finished his work during the day, he would get his book out and read. That day he finished one book, took a computer-scored test on it for comprehension, missing only one question, and began another book before the end of the day. His parent's log showed that at home in the evenings, after homework, he read or played computer games such as "Math Blaster" or "Magic School Bus" learning CDs.

The seventh grader's reward was computer time, playing computer games similar to "Jeopardy" or the new "So You Want to be a Millionaire Show." He played these with his aide, and it was fun watching their friendly competition, that at times grew loud, as the student, good naturedly, liked to try to "cheat" and hit the keys before the aide could answer correctly. His other reward was a walk around the building outside, which seemed to help him refocus when he arrived back at the classroom.

A question of mainstreaming?

As I mentioned in my Introduction, what struck me the most about these children's days were the different degrees of silence that they were happy to be in. The fourth grader would have been satisfied speaking only to his teacher, his aide and his speech therapist if it hadn't been for the fact that the aide acted almost as translator for conversations with classmates during the day. The fifth grader went almost the entire day without speaking to a classroom peer, only asking and answering questions of the teacher or aide, and, as I said, it wasn't until the last hour of the school day, when he was in the library without the aide, that another little girl worked closely with him to help him find a book. I did not observe the seventh grader speak to a peer once during his entire day. His conversations were completely with the aide or his speech therapist. Even in the cafeteria, none of the students interacted with any peers, choosing to sit by themselves and eat. At recess the two younger students didn't play with anyone else, but seemed to be completely in autism while on the playground, choosing to be on the playground equipment or swing.

Hence the question about mainstreaming comes in. Yes, these children are in the regular classroom (the seventh grader was, up until that week), but are they really being mainstreamed? One of the goals of putting these children into regular classrooms is so that they can have typical peers not only to learn social skills from, but to have the opportunity to make social connections. As a parent, I stand behind this idea and goal 100 percent. But was this what was really taking place during the day? I saw very few social interactions with any of their peers. They were in the midst of it all, yet they were still in autism. Thus my question now: how can we change this to make it a better and more productive situation for these children?

Possible conclusions

It is, of course, difficult to draw many conclusions from such an informal observation. But in addition to noticing similarities and differences, I believe I can conclude that these three students were content in their learning environments, and were all three basically happy kids. They each displayed a particular interest or talent, whether it was art, reading or computer skills, and their teachers and aides used these interests to help keep them motivated. During the day, there were minor "upsets" for each child involving entirely different things, but they were all very minor. Thus, on the surface, it seemed to me that whatever the Individual Education Plan had set out for each child, it was being implemented with some success.

Yet, even after saying all of that, this question of silence, of being able to be in a regular classroom but still in autism the majority of the time, bothered me. Thus, I came away with more questions than answers. Should we take the aides away from the students and force them to interact with their peers, as the fifth grader finally did in the library? Yes, it was a good thing for the fourth grader's aide to act as "interpreter" for the students, but will this "conversation" continue if there is no interpreter present? In addition, when looking at the smaller, special services classroom where the seventh grader had just been placed, is a BD classroom, with all of the noise and outbursts it entails, a good setting for a child with autism who generally shuts down when there is too much stimulation? Of course, each question has to be answered individually, according to each student's needs. But if I hadn't done these observations, spent these three days, I would never have had these questions, and, as you saw in Chapter 2, having questions is the best place to begin.

In the end, I felt that observing my own child was priceless. But being able to observe the other two children added an extra advantage in that I was able to note several similarities and comparisons. As a result of one day (my child was the fifth grader), we decided to withdraw the one-on-one aide beginning with sixth grade, so that, we hope, he will try to make some peer connections. Academically, Jon has so far been able to keep up with his grade level, but socially he is still two years behind. So yes, he is going into sixth grade, but he still has the social skills of a fourth grader. Maybe as a "fourth grader" he will be able to begin building tentative peer relationships? We won't know until we try, and my husband made sure to ask if we could always go back to a part-time or full-time aide if necessary. I would recommend every parent spend a day in their child's classroom, especially a parent of a child with a disability. If possible, get other parents' permission to observe their children, also. It will be an experience that you will never forget, and you too will come away full of questions, which you should then be able to answer. I for one will never forget the three days that I had to sit in silence, so that I could observe and try to understand the silence of autism. Along with everything else, I learned that Sartre is right. There is much speaking in silence.

References

MacNealy, M.S. (1999) *Strategies for Empirical Research in Writing.* Boston: Allyn & Bacon.

chicken nugget #4

Wishes and guilt

If wishes were horses, beggars might ride.
(John Ray 1670, English proverbs)

It seems like every year, right before school starts, I find myself having more wishes than usual. I wish I didn't have to try to convince my son's new teacher that I really do have some insight into autism, and especially my child's autism. I wish I didn't have to make the rounds of each teacher—PE coach, music teacher, art teacher, librarian—and give them a typewritten "Introduction to Jon" letter along with a personal invitation to join our first IEP meeting in the fall. I wish getting ready for another school year would be as simple as shopping for school supplies, attending orientation, and going to bed earlier. I wish it didn't matter who else was in my child's class, and that there weren't certain kids who for some reason "set him off" so that they couldn't be in the same class with my son. I wish my child were normal, and I wish I could escape from being an autism advocate.

Wow! I said it. Not only did I think it, but I wrote it down. Only another parent, in similar shoes, would understand my wishes, or understand the immediate guilt that follows them. Guilt, for wishing that things weren't always an extra effort when we have to get ready to start school. Guilt, for getting tired of explaining things about my child to new teachers. Guilt, for wishing my child were normal, and guilt, most of all, for wishing I could have an escape from it all.

Why is it, do you suppose, that we feel the most guilty when we are being the most honest? Is this normal parent guilt, meaning that most parents have this about their children? Or is this disability guilt, meaning as parents of disabled children we suffer a more severe type of guilt than other parents?

The only way to try to answer this is to point out that just as people grieve differently, they experience guilt differently. When my dad passed away, my three siblings and I all went through the grieving process differently. One of my sister's grief was very emotional, but as she entered the stages of grief, it seemed that she stalled out and couldn't move on. A year after his death she was in the hospital for a stress-induced mild heart attack, which could have partially been caused by that fact that she was still grieving over Dad's death. I remember talking to her on the phone while she lay in the hospital, listening to a lot of her "guilt-ridden" statements. "I *should* have called him that Sunday. I *would* have gone down to see him...I *could* have—" I interrupted her and told her that she needed to stop should-ing all over herself. (Yes, blunt, but it got her attention.) I told her that she couldn't go back and change the past, and it was useless for her to feel guilty for things that she thought she should have done while Dad was alive. Should haves, would haves, and could haves would not get her anywhere now, and to continue thinking that way would just keep her sick, grieving and guilt ridden. She tried to take my advice. At least she was soon home and back at work.

So, why can't I take my own good advice? After writing Chapter 5 on "Approaches and strategies," I mentally found myself going through my own list of should haves, would haves, could haves. There are so many interventions, treatments and methods out there, so how is a parent to know that they have really made the right choices, and done the right thing in planning their child's IEP program? I am after all just a parent trying to find the right experts and ask the right questions. What if I should have...? Ah, see how easy it is to go down that road! It takes only a second, and you are off and running, grinding yourself down into a guilt-ridden pulp. We must stop doing this to ourselves. If our children are going to succeed, we have to do the best we can, and try not to drive ourselves over the edge by wondering if we did the right thing. So, no more should haves, which *should* take care of most of the guilt.

But where does that leave wishes? I love my child more than 100 percent, if there were such a thing. But does that mean I have to love his disability? In embracing my child, I have no choice but to embrace his autism, but do I have to be happy about that? If I want to be honest with myself, no I do not have to be happy about my child's autism. I do wish that he could be like any other child who is getting ready for school. I do wish for his life to be easier. Does this wishing get me anywhere? Accomplish anything? Maybe it does. Because I believe that honestly owning up to my feelings goes a long way. For some reason, this honesty eases my guilt for even having these thoughts. Remember the little boy who did something wrong, but because he was honest and told his parents, he then felt better and was rewarded for his honesty? Maybe wishing is a waste of time and not a good thing, but at least I'm being honest. Maybe my honesty also keeps me from having ulcers, constantly sniping at my loved ones, or having the "screaming-meamies." Because I can honestly say that I wish this disability would go away, maybe I am able to embrace my son with a more open heart. Wishing doesn't change life, but it empowers us to keep going. And, every once in a while, I've seen even a beggar get a ride.

Chapter Five

Approaches and strategies
Meeting your child's needs

I begin writing this chapter almost with a sense of trepidation. Not because there is nothing we can do to help our children with autism, but because there is so much, and some of it is very controversial. Beginning in 1990 we saw a drastic increase in children being diagnosed with an autism spectrum disorder, and at the same time an increase in the various programs for treatment. What could possibly be wrong with more programs? Nothing, if we as parents are able to look at all of these programs with an optimistically pessimistic attitude. Yes, our child's autism is treatable, but a cold hard fact is that some of these programs are not scientifically based or clinically proven. Not only that, but some of them make a lot of money off parents like us who are searching for a program to help our child. What do we do? Stop searching?

If you are anything at all like me, once you felt you had a firm understanding about your child's diagnosis, you immediately began to look for ways to "fix" it. There is nothing wrong with this. It is a very normal reaction. I love and accept my child for who he is, but if I could wave a magic wand and take away this thing called autism, I would do it in a heartbeat. Unfortunately there is no magic wand, but there are numerous programs called interventions, treatments, strategies and methods. The sole purpose of these programs is to affect your child in a positive way. When my son was diagnosed, I had to wade through every program that was available to my child and make very important decisions about what we would, or would not, do to help him. Thus, my purpose in this chapter is to introduce you to what is out there by giving you the basics on each. As always, it will then be up to you to look deeper at each program, and find what will work best for your child. My dad gave me some advice when I was a young college student. It didn't have anything to do with autism, but he said, "Ann, if it looks and sounds too good to be true—it is."

Over the years, I've always tried to keep that in mind while doing my own research. Remember, no matter what the program claims, there is, as yet, no cure for autism. With this in mind, my husband and I developed an individual program for our son which continues to evolve and change throughout his life. Yes, my son can be "incognito" in that most of the time no one would ever guess that he has a disability. But he still has an autism spectrum disorder. The programs that we have used, and still use, have not "cured" him, but have helped him to function nearly normally. We have used some of the things listed in this chapter, and some we have not. But remember that you shouldn't model your program on my child's program, or any other child's. I must repeat myself that what works for one child may not work for another. So when you are reading further, yes, look into each parent's success story, but also look to see if there are any empirical data or clinical studies to support the program's claim that it produces positive results with an autism spectrum disorder. Be optimistic, but pessimistic too—even somewhat ruthless. After all, it is your child's life that will be affected.

Expert opinions

Any time I look at a subject, I feel it is always best to look to people who know more than me. Dr. Temple Grandin is not only one of our leading scientists in animal husbandry, but, more importantly for my purpose, she is high functioning autistic. I have heard her speak at two conferences, have practically devoured everything she has written on the subject of autism, and I feel she is one of the few experts who constantly gives parents the most practical advice. At a MAAP (More Advanced Individuals with Autism, Asperger's Syndrome and Pervasive Developmental Disorder/Not Otherwise Specified) conference, I wrote in my notes that she said parents should forget all of the controversy and just dedicate themselves to finding the right program to meet their child's needs. She also pointed out that she feels there is nothing wrong with using the "good" from each program when developing a program specific to the child. This made so much sense to me. After all, isn't this the purpose of an IEP? An *individual* education plan.

However, just to be on the safe side, I recently looked up Dr. Grandin's website to make sure that she still felt this way. I would highly recommend that you read the article she has posted titled "An Inside View of Autism." It is at the end of this article where she gives her views on autism programs. Grandin writes: "During my travels I have observed many different programs. It is my opinion that effective programs for young children have certain *common denominators* that are similar regardless of the theoretical basis." She goes on to reiterate that it is *intensive* early intervention programs that have the best results and that "good programs do a variety of activities and use *more than one approach*" (my emphasis). She states that when it came down to her own intervention, her governess and her mother "just used their good instincts." As always, she cautions that "a program that is effective for one case may be less effective for another". So, according to Dr. Grandin, it is an intensive program, using more than one approach, which works best, along with parents relying on their instincts to build the right program for their own child.

In addition to Dr. Grandin, another expert who is often quoted and has good advice on evaluating treatment programs is Dr. B.J. Freeman, Professor of Medical Psychology at the University of California, Los Angeles. Freeman works in the UCLA Autism Evaluation Program. Her article titled "Guidelines for Evaluating Intervention Programs for Children with Autism" was originally printed in 1992, and since then published in the *Journal of Autism and Developmental Disorders* (1997). It has also been posted, in shorter versions, on several autism/Asperger's websites. Dr. Freeman has given permission to include the updated list from her handouts "Evaluating Treatment Programs" and "Autism Spectrum Disorders: Questions Parents Ask/What We Know." I do so, because I wish I'd had it to go by when I began my own research. I'm sure it was out there, but unfortunately I didn't know where to find it. Once again, we see a list that helps us form the right questions.

Principles of evaluating treatments of autism

1. Approach any new treatment with hopeful skepticism. Remember the goal of any treatment should be to help the person with the autism become a fully functioning member of society.

2. BEWARE of any program or technique that is touted as effective or desirable for every person with autism.

3. BEWARE of any program that thwarts individualization and potentially results in harmful program decisions.

4. Be aware that any treatment other than education represents one of several options open for a person with autism.

5. Be aware that treatment should always depend on individual assessment information that points to it as an appropriate choice for a particular child.

6. Be aware that no new treatment should be implemented until its proponents can specify assessment procedures necessary to determine whether it will be appropriate for an individual with autism.

7. Be aware that debate over use of various techniques is often reduced to superficial arguments over who is right, moral and ethical, and who is a true advocate for the children.

8. Be aware that, often, new treatments have not been validated scientifically.

Questions to ask regarding specific treatment

1. What is the treatment program's rationale and purpose?

2. Is there written information?

3. What is involved for child and family?

4. What is length of treatment, frequency of sessions, time and costs to the family?

5. Does the treatment focus on one skill or is it a comprehensive program?

6. Will the treatment result in harm to the child?

7. Is the treatment developmentally appropriate?

8. What is the background and training experience of the staff?

9. Does the treatment staff allow input from the family?

10. Are assessment procedures specified and is program individualized for each child?

11. How will progress be measured?

12. How often will effectiveness of the intervention be evaluated?

13. Who will conduct the evaluation?

14. What criteria will be used to determine if a treatment should be continued or abandoned?

15. What scientific evidence supports the effectiveness of the program?

16. How will failure of treatment affect child and family?

17. How will treatment be integrated into the child's current program?

18. Do not become so infatuated with a given treatment that functional curriculum, vocational, life, and social skills are ignored.

(Freeman, March 2003)

Interventions

The Oxford English Dictionary states the definition for "intervention" as: "the action or process of intervening, and intervening as coming between, so as to prevent or alter something." Thus, interventions in autism would be for the purpose of preventing or altering the autism in a child. But since we know that an autism spectrum disorder is not going to magically go away, what are we really trying to prevent, or alter, in our child? The autism? No, the *behaviors*. Remember that autism is not diagnosed by a blood test or even a brain scan, but by looking at behaviors of the child. Therefore, it should be the goal of every intervention to try to prevent, alter or minimize behaviors that are identified in your child as autistic behaviors.

When reading through this list of interventions, realize that by the time this book goes to print there will probably be more out there, and it's possible some parents may find that I have missed what is important to them. Some of these interventions address many behaviors, while others are specific towards one behavior. They are not presented in any quality rating order, and I am determined to keep my personal opinions to myself. At the end of each, you will find places to go for further information, so that you can become the expert on the program that you will design for your child.

Behavior modification

Behavior modification means just that, modifying or changing behaviors, and has been studied in the field of psychology, and used in teaching, for years. Most parents already use behavior modification, and may not even realize it. What happens when your child misbehaves? You discipline that child in some way, whether enforcing a time out, taking away something from them, or verbally scolding them. What happens when your child does something good? Most parents give verbal praise, and sometimes that child may earn a reward such as a treat, outing or an allowance. The result of this discipline or reward is you are trying to modify your child's behavior.

In 1987, Dr. Ivor Lovaas took behavior modification one step further and applied it to autistic children, with the intention of modifying autistic behaviors. After several years of study, he reported that the greatest benefit occurred among children who received 40 hours per week of one-on-one intervention for two years. The Lovaas behavior intervention focused at first on compliance and imitation, then later moved on to repetitive and expressive language, with the final goal being integration with peers (Siegel 1996, p.202). This intervention was first called Discrete Trail (DT) and has evolved to be referred to as Intensive Behavior Intervention (IBI) and Applied Behavior Analysis (ABA).

ABA is basically implemented by using what is called the ABC model: *a*ntecedent—meaning a directive or request; *b*ehavior—the child either complies or doesn't comply; *c*onsequence—the therapist reacts with a verbal positive, or negative response. There is then a pause, and the model starts again with another ABC directive. Of course the model expands from there, as does the therapy with each child (ASA).

There have been very positive reports from parents using Lovaas's ABA intervention. You can find them posted on the internet, or in several books that have been written specifically about ABA. A few advantages of ABA are that it recognizes the need for one-on-one instruction with autistic children; uses repetition with these children until they firmly grasp the right responses; and it keeps the child actively engaged for increasing lengths of time.

One of the concerns about ABA was that in the beginning Lovaas was reported as using electric shock or spanking as physical responses to non-compliance. Dr. Byrna Siegel points out that, yes, Lovaas did do this, but it was with "severally mentally retarded children" who had "intractable self-injurious behaviors" (1996, p.203). She adds that the current ABA program does not advocate the use of negative physical responses by therapists. A few other concerns are that in some cases ABA is heavily promoted as the one and only effective program for autism, when in fact there are no comparative studies to support this claim. (There are clinical studies to show that ABA is successful, but none that compare it to other programs.) Another is that it can be overly stressful to the child because of the program's intensity, and to the family because of the prohibitive cost of approximately $50,000 per child, per year (ASA). For more specific information you may log on to www.lovaas.com or write to The Lovaas Institute, 2566 Overland Ave., Suite 530, Los Angeles, CA 90064, USA.

We did not use Lovaas's intense, 40-hour-a-week ABA with my son, but we did use ABA methods to try to reduce his autistic behaviors. Several times, his aide, I, or possibly another teacher would see a behavior that, if reduced, or even eliminated, would benefit my son. In those cases, a specific behavior assessment form was filled out, and a method devised to try to effect a positive outcome. This individualized ABA worked for my son, and still does.

TEACCH

This stands for Treatment and Education of Autistic and related Communication-handicapped Children. TEACCH has been around for over 32 years and has empirical data to support the strength of its approach. The difference between TEACCH and ABA is that the focus is on autism rather than behavior. The main goal of TEACCH is to provide *strategies* and *supports* so that the autistic person can experience success throughout the lifespan. This goal is implemented by organizing and modifying the environments and activities of the autistic individual; emphasizing visual and functional learning; and basing curriculum on individualized assessments (ASA).

Many parents may be using this intervention with their children without being aware of what it's called. After all, isn't it probably a goal of every parent to have the child develop the ability to move comfortably through the school system, and into the community, using supports and modifications where necessary? Some of the successes of this program are reported to be improved adaptation of the individual, and an increase in functional skills. In North Carolina (where the program was originally implemented), reports show the lowest account of parental stress and a higher success rate of autistic individuals finding employment. Another positive is that this method incorporates and uses all of the other strategies that the child may be using such as Picture Exchange Communication System (PECS), occupational therapy, physical therapy and many others.

Some of the concerns regarding this approach are that it "gives in" to autism because it doesn't try to change autistic behaviors, but makes *adaptations* that allow for autism (ASA). Others who are opposed to this method say that this intervention doesn't bring children into a "normal" society, but isolates them even more by failing to help them develop "normal" social skills. More information can be found at www.TEACCH.com or by writing to TEACCH Division of University North Carolina, 310 Medical School, Wing E, CB #7180, Chapel Hill, NC 27599–7180, USA.

We use the TEACCH intervention, also, in adapting our son's environment either at home or in the classroom by providing him with supports to help him function in a "normal" society. Our goal is for our son to be able to reduce autistic behaviors, but we also don't want him to be miserable. So if a modification is needed to help ease the situation, we do it. At this point, yes, we are giving into his autism, but he is autistic.

PECS

PECS stands for Picture Exchange Communication System, and emphasizes the difference between talking and communicating. Combined with speech therapy, this method works to help a child who is not typically attaching meaning to words. The goals of PECS are to help the child spontaneously to initiate communication, understand the function of communication, and then to develop communicative competency. In very young children, this method begins with rewards specific to the child's interests, and later on grows to more social rewards (ASA).

Some of the advantages of this intervention are that it is well suited for pre-verbal and non-verbal children, and for children with a higher performance IQ than a verbal IQ. There is also empirical data that show an increased communicative competency after PECS, in that children actually are understanding the function of communication.

One concern seems to be that the training for the therapist is minimal, and that this could disrupt the method. On top of that, because of the concern about lack of training, it is also possible that the method is then used too inconsistently within the classroom to even prove beneficial (ASA). More information can be found on the "founders" website at www.pecs.com or by writing to Pyramid Educational Consultants, 226 West Park Place, Suite 1, Newark, DE 19711, USA.

We have never used PECS with my son's program. But one day when I observed another autistic child, I was allowed to go to speech therapy with him, where the speech teacher used PECS. It was a very easy flash card method, and during the 30 minutes there were two or three instances in which the picture not only brought out the correct response from the child, but a spontaneous social exchange occurred.

Inclusion

It was surprising to see inclusion listed as an intervention, but I suppose it could be considered as such. This, of course, is where the disabled child is "mainstreamed" into the regular classroom, and it evolved from Federal Laws 94–142, REI (Regular Education Initiative) and IDEA (Individuals with Disabilities Education Act). Originally it was set up to address mental retardation and other disabilities, not autism. Inclusion's goal is to educate the child with "normal" children in the regular classroom either half day or full day, with the belief that it gives more opportunities for role modeling, social interaction, and exposure to verbal communication. At the same time, inclusion gives the neurotypical (NT) peers a better understanding and tolerance of differences in others (ASA).

The advantages would be great for the autistic child if indeed they achieved any of the above mentioned goals; i.e., learning from better role modeling and social interaction, with the result of showing a marked benefit in being exposed to normal verbal communication.

The concerns with this approach are that some see inclusion as an "automatic" placement for a disabled child, and that this then defeats the whole purpose of "individual" placement of each child in the "best and least restrictive environment" which is the basis of IDEA. Another concern is that the regular classroom teachers, along with the students, are sometimes ill prepared to receive an autistic student into their classooms. This would result in no benefit at all for the individual student, or for the class (ASA). There are several places on the internet for more information on inclusion: www.inclusion.org or www.circleofinclusion.org (for birth to age eight), or you may write to The Inclusion Network, 312 Walnut Str., Cincinnati, OH 45202, USA.

My son has always been "mainstreamed" for a full day in the regular classroom. He has also always had a one-on-one classroom aide. In sixth grade the aide was no longer used, but there was a second teacher, for half the day, who had several students, up to five, within the classroom who had IEPs. She acted as a "team" teacher with the regular classroom teacher. Thus, up to this point in Jon's life, inclusion has worked. If ever it gets to the point where inclusion is no longer benefiting him, we will consider taking him out and finding another solution. Our program evolves yearly as my son's needs change.

Social stories

Social stories, or social scripts, were developed in 1991 by Carol Gray (2000). At first, they were to teach children with a diagnosis of autism the "rules of the game." But since then they have developed into more elaborate stories and scripts to teach NT behavior by addressing issues of an NT culture, and attempting to teach autistic children to see another person's perspective. This intervention is implemented by writing a story for the child, which can be as simple or as elaborate as needed. An example would be if the child is going to be experiencing something he/she has never done before, such as a bus ride to school. The script may be similar to the following:

> After I eat my breakfast tomorrow morning, my mom will take me outside to wait for the bus ride to school. If it is raining, we can wait inside. If it is nice, I will stand in the driveway, around the time that the bus will come up my street to pick me up. The bus driver will stop his bus in front of my driveway, and slowly the door will open. I must wait until the bus is stopped and standing still before I can approach it. After the door opens, I can then climb aboard, using the handrail to pull myself up the steps. If I slip on the step, it is okay. Sometimes other kids slip and they just pull themselves up into the bus. The bus driver will tell me good morning and say something like, "Have a seat, please." I will sit down on the first empty seat. I can look around at the other students on the bus, but I cannot stand up or leave my seat. This is one of the rules. No moving from my seat or standing up once I am on the bus. The bus trip will not take very long, but it may feel like a long time to me, as the bus stops several more times to pick up other students. I can read my book that is in my backpack if I want to. When the bus arrives at school, and after it stops at the curb, I must wait my turn to get off of the bus. The kids in the front of the bus will stand up and get off first. I must wait until each seat in front of me is empty before it is my turn. I will tell the bus driver "Have a good day!" and climb down the steps, holding the railing. Then I will go straight inside the school and to my classroom.

As you can see by my impromptu story, the goal is to provide a script explaining step by step what will happen to the child, and the behavior that is expected of the child for this specific situation.

One of the benefits of using social stories is that it prepares the child for the event, which then reduces the anxiety and stress level of the child. If used consistently, the social story could nip any problem behavior in the bud. Another benefit is that this intervention was developed specifically for autistic children to overcome social deficits, and that it is cost

efficient, flexible, and can be tailored to each individual's level of understanding and communication (ASA).

   One of the concerns is that the success of this method is anecdotal
rather than empirical, and for the method to have a benefit, it depends on
the skills of the writer writing the social story for the child. There are
also opponents that point out that the writer is trying to take on the
perspective of the autistic child, and that this is more difficult than
one may think (ASA). More on social stories can be found at
www.thegraycenter.org/social.html or by writing to The Gray Center,
PO Box 67, Jenison, MI 49429, USA.

   When my son was younger, his aide and I wrote out many social
stories, short or elaborate, whatever was needed for the occasion. Now
that he is older, we take the time to "talk out" what will happen and what
behavior is expected of him. Because it isn't written down, I sometimes
have to go over and over it, but it works the same as a social story.

Treatment approaches

I have grouped treatment approaches separately from interventions.
Treatment approaches are different ways of looking at a diagnosis of
autism spectrum disorder, which then dictate the type of treatment used.
Once again, these are listed here to give you the basics, so that you can
research what would work best for your child.

Neurological approach (the brain-injured child)

The Institutes for the Achievement of Human Potential have been
operating since the 1960s and are still controversial. Based on the book
by Glenn Doman and David Melton (1994), *What to Do About Your
Brain-Injured Child*, the Institutes' approach is that "autism is not a
diagnosis but rather a description of one symptom of a brain-injured
child who is usually injured in the cortical and midbrain areas of the
brain" (IAHP Report). In this treatment, the parents of the child first take
a course at the institute, based on Doman's various methods of "pattern-
ing" physical and mental behavior. They then set up a home-based
program to work with their child in hopes of "repairing" the brain.

   This program was not originally set up to work with autism spectrum
disorders, but they now use several methods toward their goal of making
autistic children well children (IAHP, Bronson). Although one clinical

study was published on the study of cross-patterning (to promote more effective movement), two of the methods used are not as yet backed by empirical data. These are auditory training, where the child's brain is retrained to have normal range auditory response, as opposed to hypo or hyper responses, and facilitated communication, where the child who is non-verbal uses a communication board to point to words, or spell out words, in order to communicate.

Many parents from all over the world have read Glenn Doman's books, and have brought their children to the Institutes. There are parents reporting not only success with their brain-injured children, but "cures" for their previously autistic children (IAHP, Bronson).

Two of the concerns are the cost and the intensity of this program. Many parents report experiencing very high stress levels, burn out, and sometimes financial catastrophe. Other opponents point to the fact that replication of auditory training in clinical studies has not proved that this method benefits an autistic child. In addition, facilitated communication in clinical study, where the parent or facilitator holds the child's hand on the communication wand, has shown that the facilitator may unknowingly be directing the child's hand (Herbert and Sharp 2000). More information can be found at the Institutes' website www.iahp.org or by writing to them at the Institutes for the Achievement of Human Potential, 8801 Stanton Ave., Philadelphia, PA 19038, USA.

I had not heard of IAHP until working with one of my college professors. His family has had success with the Institutes' programs in setting up a program for their daughter, along with other combined interventions.

Biomedical approach

The Autism Research Institute (ARI), founded by Bernard Rimland, looks at autism biologically. In fact, Rimland was one of the first to point out that autism was not a psychological disorder, but biological. Because of this belief, Rimland began performing tests on autistic individuals by giving them high doses of vitamin B6. It is the Institute's belief that large doses of B6 and magnesium combine to reduce autistic symptoms and "normalize body metabolism" (Rimland 1996a). In the literature it is stated that "vitamin B6 makes the child *more normal* in *many* ways" (Rimland 1996a, p.2, author's emphasis).

More recently, Rimland has also begun using secretin in the treatment of autism. ARI states that it does not know for sure how it works, but believes that because secretin receptors are involved in so many areas of the brain and nervous system, the increased secretin could possibly affect the brain directly (Rimland 1996b).

DMG (dimethyglycine), a food supplement, is also reported by the ARI as being helpful in the treatment of autism. It is reported to increase energy, boost the immune system, and increase eye contact while reducing frustration levels (Rimland 1996c).

Many of the success stores of B6, DMG and secretin are anecdotal, and although there have been several clinical tests and studies on these three treatments and their effects on autism, there is not yet any scientific evidence to prove the ARI's claims (Herbert and Sharp 2000). More information can be found at www.autism.com/ari/contents.html or by writing to The Autism Research Institute, 4182 Adams Ave., San Diego, CA 92116, USA.

I first looked into Rimland's methods when my son was diagnosed, and the ARI sent me packets of information. I did not go with their program at that time, but when the secretin method came out, I also studied it. Parents will have to make up their own minds on this issue.

Dietary approach

This approach stresses that autism is exacerbated by a child's allergic reaction to certain foods in their diets. As of yet there are no rigorous scientific studies to support the belief that dietary modification is effective in reducing or eliminating the symptoms of autism.

Gluten-free/casein-free diet

Several books and parent organizations support the belief that autistic children have trouble digesting gluten (found in wheat, barley, oats and rye), and casein (found in dairy products). As a result of problems digesting gluten and casein, the peptides that remain at high levels in the stomach leak out into the blood system and cause a certain reaction in the brain at the point that is called opioid receptors. According to Dr. William Shaw, one of the proponents of this belief, once these peptides get to the brain, because they haven't been properly digested, they act like heroin or morphine and affect congnitive abilities, emotions, pain thresholds, sound sensitivity, and areas of the brain that are involved with speech and auditory integration (Hamilton 2000, pp.117–118). After an allergy test is done on the child, the belief is that once these foods are removed from the child's diet, autistic symptoms will be greatly reduced. More information can be found on this particular diet at www.gfcdiet.com or writing to a parent organization at ANDI, PO Box 335, Pennington, NJ 08534–0335, USA.

The only dietary intervention that we have done with our son was that very early on we took him off milk. My husband is lactose intolerant and my son seemed to show symptoms of the same condition. Also, it seemed to us and his teachers that when he had milk for breakfast and lunch he was slower to process information during the day, had trouble staying focused and got upset a lot easier. So, we took him off milk (he doesn't like cheese and still ate vanilla ice cream once in a while), and he took an over-the-counter multivitamin plus calcium. Just recently, he has started having a very small amount of milk again on his cereal, and we haven't noticed any change in behavior. I understand that food allergies also evolve during a person's life, and I wonder if this is the case with him.

Anti-yeast diet

Dr. Semon, a child psychiatrist, nutritionist, and parent of a child with autism, co-authored a book in which he describes how it is his belief that many autistic children struggle with yeast (candida albicans) overgrowth in their systems. Dr. Semon believes that it is necessary to eliminate a very long list of foods for two reasons: one, these foods contain chemicals that kill bacteria and act as low-level antibiotics; two, these foods contain chemicals that slow down the brain (Hamilton 2000, p.134). Hence, according to Semon, if these foods are completely elimi-nated, the brain functions better and autistic symptoms are reduced. More information on this can be found on ARI's website, specifically at http://autism.org/candida.html.

I ate lunch with a mother at a conference once who had just put her child on this diet, plus the gluten-free/casein-free diet. She was very excited about it and told everyone at the table that we all must do the same, or we were slowly poisoning our children, and keeping them autistic. This is another issue that we all must honestly look into for ourselves.

Medications

There are, as yet, no specific medications to treat autism, but some are prescribed to alleviate certain symptoms, such as aggression, seizures, hyperactivity, obsessive/compulsive behaviors or anxiety (ASA). There are several good sites that address many of the previous issues, along with medications. One is www.autism-biomed.org or the address is ABINET, PO Box 1292, Highland Park, IL 60035, USA. This site is very up to date, and is posted by Dr. Ronald J. Kallen, MD.

So far, Jon has not had to have any medications. At one conference I attended a session on "Psycho-pharmaceuticals." The specialist, a trained psychiatrist who also worked with individuals with autism spectrum disorders, spent over an hour going through what drugs could help the "symptoms" that our children are having. He gave us drug charts, we all took rapid notes, and in the end one thing he said brought it all together. When I asked him whether a child with an autism spectrum disorder should be medicated, he replied, "Only if there are behaviors in his/her life that are affecting the quality of life, by disrupting the person's ability to attend school or function in the home." I am hoping that Jon can remain med-free.

Your approach

There are many more interventions, treatments and approaches out there. I have only scraped the tip of the iceberg. There are also music therapy, vision therapy, sensory integration, and detoxification. My list could go on and on, and still there would be something that I might have missed. What I hope I have done is to give you a crash course on the basics, so that now you are an informed parent who has some of the groundwork laid, and is able to build the right "program" for your child. As you do so, remember the advice from the experts about evaluating and building autism programs, and remember to go with your gut instincts and parental common sense.

In my approach, I really am very optimistic when I hear about new interventions, treatments or methods. One day there may be a real break-through that will make my child's life easier. But as I read and study each new program, I can't forget my dad's advice: "If it looks and sounds too good to be true—it is."

References

Autism Society of America (ASA) "Autism Treatments." www.autism-society.org (2001, 11 June)

Doman, G. and Melton, D. (1994) *What to Do About Your Brain-Injured Child.* Garden City Park: Avery Pub. Group.

Freeman, B.J. (2003) "Evaluating Treatment Programs" and "Autism Spectrum Disorders: Questions Parents Ask/What We Know." Handouts, UCLA School of Medicine.

Grandin, T. "An Inside View of Autism." Center for the Study of Autism. www.autism.org/temple/inside.html (2001, 17 June).

Gray, C. (2000) *The New Social Story Book.* Arlington: Future Horizons.

Hamilton, L.M. (2000) *Facing Autism.* Colorado Springs: Waterbrook Press.

Herbert, J.D. and Sharp, I.R. (2000) "Pseudoscientific Treatments for Autism, Part 1 and Part 2." American Council on Science and Health, September & October. www.drkoop.com/news/focus/september/autism.html and www.drkoop.com/news/focus/october/autism.html (2001, 11 June).

Institutes for the Achievement of Human Potential (IAHP) "Bronson Tate – From 'Autism' to Wellness." http://iahp.org/hurt/children/bronson_tate.html (2001, 19 June)

Institutes for the Achievement of Human Potential (IAHP) "The Institutes Report on Autism." http://iahp.org/institutes_report/autism/indes.html (2001, 19 June).

Oxford English Dictionary (1999) Oxford: Oxford University Press.

Rimland, B. (1996a) *Form Letter Regarding High Dosage Vitamin B6 and Magnesium Therapy for Autism.* Bethesda, MA: Autism Society of America.

Rimland, B. (1996b) *Defeat Autism Now.* San Diego: Autism Research Institute.

Rimland, B. (1996c) *Dimethyiglycine (DMG) For Autism.* San Diego: Autism Research Institute.

Siegel, B. (1996) *The World of the Autistic Child.* New York: Oxford Press.

chicken nugget #5

The important relationship between a sense of humor and your sanity

The human race has one really effective weapon, and that is laughter.

(Mark Twain)

Humor is to life what shock absorbers are to automobiles.

(Unknown)

How many times have we heard the expression "I laughed to keep from crying." I found so many famous and infamous thoughts on humor and laugher that it was hard to choose whom to quote. In the end I chose Twain because I too firmly believe that "laughter is a weapon." I don't think I would be here without a sense of humor, and I don't think I could survive what the future might bring if I lost it.

After my son's diagnosis and before the next school year began, a group of educators and I attended a three-day seminar on autism. The group consisted of the special services director for the small school district we were in, my son's soon-to-be teacher, his soon-to-be aide, and the speech teacher whom he would be working with. It was at this first seminar where I learned that a sense of humor can get you through.

There were a total of six of us that drove up from our small town to a larger city to attend the conference, and the school district allowed me to be the "free" person on their reservation. (Many conferences allow the fifth or sixth person from the school district to attend free of charge.) I was just coming out of shock after my child's diagnosis, trying to move into acceptance at the time, and I had no idea what to expect at this conference. I felt relatively comfortable with the educators. We had been through a lot since my son's diagnosis a few months before, and I trusted that they had my child's best interests at heart.

When we arrived at the school where the seminar was being held, I immediately felt overwhelmed by the attendance; not just how many had shown up—they had to add 50 extra chairs—but who had shown up. The first speaker asked for a show of hands of who was in attendance, teachers, aides, speech teachers, administrators, and when she got to parents there were only five of us out of two hundred or so.

The day began, and the first speaker immediately set the tone for the next few days. She was looking for a set of overheads, and as she was talking and walking around with the mike, she kept looking. Finally she stopped speaking and looked out at us. "I suppose you all are wondering why I'm worrying about this right now, at this moment, when I won't need these overheads until right before lunch." She smiled and shook her head. "I'm sorry, I'm having an autistic moment. I can't focus on the present because I'm worried about an hour from now." There was light laughter in the audience. "And, I'm being slightly obsessive compulsive because if I don't have my overheads in plain view I can't go on with this morning's session!" More laughter. Finally, one of the other speakers helped her locate her overheads and placed them where she needed them so she could go on.

After those opening remarks, the rest of the day continued in the same vein. I don't remember every detail—I wish I could—but I do remember that each speaker used humor in her presentation, which resulted in putting everyone in the room at ease. By humor, I don't mean crassness or sick humor, but humor in that although we all knew that autism was a serious subject, we began to learn that laughter was one way to keep from shedding too many tears.

This camaraderie and sense of humor slipped over into the small group I was with, and we had the most informative and fun three days that I can remember. On the last day, one of the speakers decided that perhaps she owed the audience a possible explanation about the way this conference had turned out. It seems that all of this humor was not typical of one of their conferences. She went on to explain that just recently her own child had been diagnosed with a severe sensory integration disorder. Suddenly she began weeping and she explained that she, a disability educator, had not noticed that her daughter's sensory issues could be more than just normal childhood finickiness. She related how when she helped her then three-year-old brush her teeth, she would cry and complain that it hurt so much that she didn't want to brush her teeth. The same thing happened with brushing her hair. It wasn't until just recently that she had learned that her daughter had a sensory disorder, and she was devastated that she hadn't been able to figure out what was going on sooner.

There wasn't a dry eye in the house after she finished speaking. One of the other speakers took over and continued by explaining that the night before, at dinner, they had realized that this was probably why humor had entered so much into this conference. They thought that perhaps they were all feeling their colleague's pain, and were dealing with this pain through humor. But they wanted us to know that autism, any disability, is of course, a serious subject, and they hoped they hadn't offended anyone, especially the few parents in attendance. When they wrapped things up a few minutes later, I raised my hand to make a comment. I told them who I was, and that I had just experienced the most informative three days of my life in this introduction to autism seminar. I also said that if it hadn't been for the sometimes wacky sense of humor that had been present, I would have been entirely overwhelmed by some of the subject matter, and might have gone home very depressed. What they had shared with me, besides important information, was the knowledge that sometimes we have to laugh to keep from crying and that a sense of humor goes a long way to easing not only the stress of a moment, but of a lifetime. I, for one, had not been offended, and I thanked them for their honesty in showing me that sometimes laughter is our best weapon.

Afterthoughts

> Don't tug on superman's cape. Don't spit into the wind.
> Don't pull the mask off of the 'ole lone ranger and don't
> mess around with Jim!
>
> *(Jim Croce)*

Because this nugget is on humor, I had to put my favorite Jim Croce song lyric in and tell you why this lyric relates to my son. Over the years, we have learned that because of Jon's autism, common sense is not one of his strong points. Croce's lyrics are obvious to others (of course you would do none of the above), but not if you are my son. Unfortunately, Jon would be one of the few to do all of the above.

There are too many incidents to try to keep track of, but a recent one comes to mind. During the past few years of school, both of my son's music directors have realized that Jon has a great memory and loves performing. So each year he has auditioned and been given speaking parts in the musicals. This year's musical was an adaptation of *Treasure Island*, and Jon's part didn't come until the very end, as he was the pirate that had been left on the island to "guard the treasure." The evening's performance was going all right, but it was hot in the gymnasium, and the children singing and speaking seemed to have lost their enthusiasm for what they were doing. One could sense in the audience a bit of restlessness and slight boredom. When it came to the part where the characters arrive on the island to find the buried treasure, my husband started video taping. A group of children came out to meet the other children on the stage. My son wasn't among them, and I felt a moment of dread. But suddenly I heard chuckles, and there was my son, arriving slightly late for his cue, hurrying into the middle of the group. He turned and faced the audience, gave us a big wave and a smile, and delivered his first line, "I be Ben Gunn!" The audience responded with laughter at the way he had suddenly taken center stage, and he grinned even more. For the next few minutes the children delivered their lines, and my son's excitement and enthusiasm brought instant life back into the play. The audience laughed a few more times and clapped when he finished speaking. Later on, when many parents and teachers came up to me to tell me what a great job Jon had done, I could only think of one thing, "Comic relief." Without knowing it, my son's open enjoyment of being in front of the crowd had brought laughter to the audience and had "saved the play" from dying a slow death.

When Jon saw himself on videotape that night, he was instantly upset and apologetic that he had broken the cardinal rule by "waving at the audience." Evidently this was one thing that the music director had told them they could not do. I told him he had done just fine, and everyone had liked his part, and it was no big deal that he had waved. I didn't tell him that the play had been too boring up to that point, but several other parents had told us just that.

One thing I know for sure: my son has autistic moments, and he also has very funny moments. Sometimes the two are related, and sometimes they aren't. But just because he has a disability doesn't mean we can't laugh—with him, or at something he does. Not surprisingly, one of his compulsive interests right now, besides the current Digimon or Disney, is jokes and riddles. He loves making them up and retelling them. Some of them are really awful, and some are just plain funny. We keep telling him that he needs to start writing them down, so here are a few.

Jon's jokes

What do you call a con-artist who is a psychiatrist?
Sigmund Fraud. "Get it?" Jon says. "Fr*aud* not Fr*eud*?"

What do you call a Digimon that has a bad odor?
Stinkmon. "Instead of Stingmon, the true evolved form of Wormon." (Have to be really up on Digimon to get that one!)

What is a pig's favorite karate move?
Porkchop!

What are the Gingerbread Man's favorite martial arts?
Judough and *Taekwondough.* "Both *dough*, get it?"

What do you get when you cross a fruit and a famous writer?
Shakespear! "Get it, Shake*spear*, as in *pears*?"

Okay, enough with the jokes. Sometimes, of course, they are not as funny in print! A few other places to find great humor to help you get through life are R. Wayne Gilpin's books *Laughing & Loving with Autism, More Laughing & Loving with Autism* and *Much More Laughing and Loving with Autism.* All are published by Future Horizons and are well worth your time. There is also a newsletter which I don't remember how I found out about, but I was a card carrying member for six years. *Brimstone Bulletin* is put out by the group Mothers From Hell 2. This group of ladies can be found on their website at www.mothersfromhell2.org. They have a great, slightly warped, sense of humor, and are also a very caring group of people who are trying to do good for children with disabilities. This joke is from one of their recent newsletters, along with the comment that maybe this is why it takes so long for bureaucracy to change things.

How many school administrators does it take to change a lightbulb?

Number unknown: One to design the lightbulb removal program; one to write the lightbulb intervention plan; one to write the drop-out prevention plan; and one to act as a lightbulb administrator to make sure nobody else tries to change the lightbulb while planning goes on. Every other administrator will be agitating against the change to come.

I do realize that sometimes we can't laugh. Sometimes something happens that we simply cannot turn into a chuckle, but I can't get this quote out of my mind by Mahatma Gandhi: "If I had no sense of humor, I would long ago have committed suicide." How important my sense of humor is to me!

Chapter Six

More resources than you can shake a stick at!

Call me overly cautions or just plain compulsive (I've been called both in many IEP meetings), but if I'm going to give you a list of books and resources, I want to have read the book and know that the resource is dependable. Thus, the following lists are of books that I have read and resources that I have contacted, in some way, myself. I could easily fatten up this chapter by listing every book or source out there on autism, but I don't want to confuse you like that. I've tried to put things in a logical order, but I do realize that my logic may not match someone else's. Feel free to pick and choose, and begin your reading and research wherever you are inclined.

Books for beginning

- *Crossing Bridges: A Parent's Perspective on Coping After a Child is Diagnosed with Autism/PDD*, by Roxanne Campbell, Barbara Peerenboom and Viki Satkiewicz-Gayhardt (1996, PUP Foundation). This book is written by several parents of children with an autism spectrum disorder. It is easy to read, very informative, and inspirational. I purchased copies of this one for my family members when my son was first diagnosed.

- *Thinking in Pictures: And Other Reports from My Life with Autism*, by Temple Grandin (1995, Doubleday). I can't say enough about this book. It will give you wonderful insights into the "possible" way that your child is thinking (remembering that no two autistics are alike). And if you really want expert advice, there is no better than Dr. Grandin.

- *A Parent's Guide to Autism: Answers to the Most Common Questions*, by Charles A. Hart (1993, Pocket Books). This was the first book that I picked up and read in that bookstore so long ago. It is still current and still considered the "essential handbook for understanding your child's needs" (cover blurb). I made our local library order two copies.

- *The World of the Autistic Child*, by Byrna Siegel (1996, Oxford University Press). This is one of the books that was a little "over my head" when I started reading it. But the more I read, the more I understood. This is a great reference book, something you will be glad you can refer back to for a long time.

Books for more specific needs

- *Asperger's Syndrome: A Guide to Parents and Professionals*, by Tony Attwood (1998, Jessica Kingsley Publishers). As Charles Hart's book has become the bible on autism, this is surely the bible on Asperger's Syndrome. Attwood writes in a very organized and understandable manner. I bought this as my son grew older, and we began to realize he might have Asperger's Syndrome rather than be autistic.

- *Higher Functioning Adolescents and Young Adults with Autism*, by Ann Fullerton, Joyce Stratton, Phyllis Coyne and Carol Gray (1996, Pro-Ed). This book is a rather expensive "teacher's guide" but I bought it to pass on to my son's future teachers, as he goes into the upper grades. It has a great section on adapting instructions or materials, and teaching self-organization and time management. (Gee, I could use a little of that myself.)

- *I Openers: Parents Ask Questions About Sexuality with Children with Developmental Disabilities*, by Dave Hingsburger (1993, Family Support Institute Press, Canada). I bought this little book when I attended a conference on autism/Asperger's and adolescent sexuality. It was a subject that I had been in denial about. However, I am thankful that I did finally face it. Sexuality is just another issue that we as parents must deal with. We just have to deal with it differently than other parents.

- *Asperger Syndrome: A Guide for Education and Parents,* by Brenda Smith Myles and Richard L. Simpson (1998, Pro-Ed). This book is a great resource full of charts, forms and outlines on teaching academic content to children with Asperger's Syndrome, or for planning for success after school. We aren't at that transition stage yet, but I always want to be ahead of things.

- *Asperger Syndrome and Rage,* by Brenda Smith Myles and Jack Southwick (1999, Autism Asperger Publications). This book was a lifesaver when my son began to get frustrated or angry at school, and strike out at whoever was standing nearby. I passed it around to every member of the IEP team and made them sign off after they read it. (Yes, compulsive, I know.)

- *Autism and Learning: A Guide to Good Practice,* edited by Stuart Powell and Rita Jordan (1997, David Fulton). This book is compiled by specialists in the UK. The reason I like it is that it gives great ideas that perhaps educators in the USA haven't attempted. I specifically purchased it for the chapters on teaching science, and therapy with computers.

Books that not only informed me, but have nourished my soul

- *Eating an Artichoke,* by Echo R. Fling (2000, Jessica Kingsley Publishers). This is Echo's story of her son's diagnosis and struggle. She faced a lot of the same things we all face, and she kept a sense of humor too.

- *Asperger Syndrome, the Universe and Everything,* by Kenneth Hall (2001, Jessica Kingsley Publishers). This book, written by a very advanced, bright, witty boy of ten, who just happens to have Asperger's Syndrome, is a must for every parent. His comments on life interspersed with the interests of a child amazed me.

- *From the Heart: On Being the Mother of a Child with Special Needs*, edited by Jane D.B. Marsh (1995, Woodbine House). This book was written by parents in a support group. It is the first book that I allowed myself to read on this topic, being a mom of a special needs child. I used up an entire box of tissues as I read other moms' stories, but I came away refreshed, renewed and somehow repaired. My heart had been broken, but these stories helped to repair it.

- *News From the Border*, by Jane Taylor McDonnell and Paul McDonnell (1997, Black Willow Press). This book, written mostly by Jane, tells the story of Paul's early life, diagnosis, and later his struggles with independence as a young adult. Paul writes the Preface and Afterword, and I learned from his pages about my own son's possible future, as a young man who is also high functioning autistic.

- *An Anthropologist on Mars*, by Oliver Sacks (1995, Alfred A. Knopf). This book tells seven stories of people with neurological disabilities. Temple Grandin is the anthropologist from Mars. After reading this story about the time that Dr. Sacks spent with Dr. Grandin, I feel that I know her personally, although I realize that because of Dr. Grandin's autism and desire for privacy, this feeling would probably bother her. But I found it amazing that Sacks seemed to get so close.

Books that made me laugh

- *Laughing & Loving with Autism, More Laughing & Loving with Autism* and *Much More Laughing and Loving with Autism*, all compiled by R. Wayne Gilpin (1993, 1994, 2003, Future Horizons). These are full of real-life anecdotes, not only about Gilpin's son Alex, but also stories sent in by other parents. Face it, our children are funny, and do very funny things. Some of them are connected to their autism, some not. All are short and very quick reads.

Organizations that I have relied upon

- Autism, Asperger Resource Center (AARC), University of Kansas Medical Center, 4001 HC, Miller Building, 3901 Rainbow Boulevard, Kansas City, KS 66160–7335, USA (www.kumc.edu/aarc/). I connected with this organization for more information on high functioning autism/ Asperger's. They organize short conferences and are always current with the most recent information.

- Autism Society of America (ASA), 7910 Woodmont Avenue, Suite 300, Bethesda, MD 20814–3067, USA (www.autism-society.org). This was the very first organization I joined, and I will always be thankful that I did. For members they publish *The Advocate*, a newsletter that outshines all others. The ASA is very responsible when it comes to passing on information, and I feel that they would never knowingly steer a parent wrong. I recommend this group without hesitation.

- MAAP Services, Inc. (More Advanced Individuals with Autism, Asperger Syndrome, and Pervasive Developmental Disorder/Not Otherwise Specified), PO Box 524, Crown Point, IN 46308, USA (www.maapservices.org). This organization publishes the newsletter *The MAAP* to its members. It is stuffed full of letters from parents, individuals with autism spectrum disorders, and articles from professionals in the field. They do their best to help, answer questions, and also organize great conferences.

- Mothers From Hell 2, PO Box 19, German Valley, IL 61039, USA (www.mothersfromhell2.org). This was the second organization that I joined, and their name tells it all. The newsletter *Brimstone Bulletin*, published for members, is the highlight of my month. These fellow mothers make me laugh, cry, and most importantly make me feel that I am not alone. In between the wacky sense of humor is real help for those of us who can always use it.

- Project ACCESS, 901 S. National Avenue, Springfield, MO 65804–0088, USA (www.smsu.edu/access/). This is

Missouri's office on autism and pervasive developmental disorders. Many states have similar offices, sometimes under the same moniker of ACCESS. If you don't find one listed in this way, your state will have an office on special education. I contacted ACCESS after I had gone through denial about my child's diagnosis, and was finally ready to learn everything I could. They sent me, literally, a box full of information, and were always available for any questions I had. Thankfully, they are still available, as my questions continue to change.

Information on the World Wide Web

Of course doing a subject search on autism on the internet is where you will find a lot more information, but as I was writing this resource chapter I realized that if I listed a lot of websites, by the time this book came to print, it was possible those sites may have changed. So, instead of listing hundreds of sites I would like to remind you of one thing. *Anyone* can post *any* information on the internet. What does this mean to us as parents? Surf the web cautiously. It can be a goldmine of information on autism, but it can also be a dangerous pit if you believe the wrong information. Yes, of course, you will benefit greatly from the internet, but post this next to your computer: *Just because you find it on the internet, doesn't make it so.*

chicken nugget #6

Something we must have—courage

Courage: the ability to do something that frightens one.

(The Oxford English Dictionary)

What do they got, that I ain't got? Courage!

(Jack Haley as the Lion in The Wizard of Oz)

There are many things parents go through in life that require an almost superhuman strength. Although I have looked through every one of my clothes closets, I can't find a red cape with a big "S" on it. Therefore, I sometimes have to knuckle down, grit my teeth, and along with the Lion from *OZ*, yell, "Courage!" as I go forward.

One unforgettable moment was when I took my son to a preschool for the very first time. His grandmother had been his babysitter up until age three, but when we moved to a different state it was either find a sitter or stay at home. (Having worked outside the home my entire life, I couldn't see myself staying at home.) I remember finding a Dr. Seuss book bag and getting a bright red lunch box with his name on it. I packed his favorite two books, a picture book of dinosaurs and a Sesame Street ABC book, and for lunch his dinosaur-shaped chicken nuggets (truthfully, they had them then), along with a few of the tiny boxes of raisins. We didn't know about our son's autism at this time, but we knew he was a picky eater.

Soon, I was dropping him at the lady's home who ran a small preschool for up to ten children. Jon and I had visited before, I had checked out her references and state licenses, and although my stomach was in knots, I knew this was a good thing for him. What surprised me was that he didn't even cry when I left him. He was too busy exploring all of the new toys and had found his favorite thing, a whole stack of wooden puzzles.

No, he didn't cry, but I did. I cried all the way across town to my new job. I remember telling myself that he would be all right and asking myself: how is a small child supposed to learn that when his mommy leaves him, she will be back, if it isn't experienced first hand? At that time, the only thing that got me out of the car and into the office building was—courage!

Switch to a much later time of life. Jon is ten years old and wants to go to a local summer camp for a week. We know all about his autism now and have spoken at length with the small camp to make sure everyone who will be working with him understands his special needs. They are very cooperative and allow me to send his own food to the camp cafeteria, so this is one hurdle we don't have to deal with. I help him pack his small duffel bag, and along with the Pokemon and Digimon dictionaries (his latest compulsion), he packs his blanket that he still sleeps with. I wonder about this, but he doesn't seem worried at all that the kids will make fun of him.

All too soon, I am dropping him at the camp. They have assigned a young man to be with him, almost one on one the entire week. We have met him already and he has explained to us that he grew up with a friend next door who is like my son. Jon sees this new friend, and is so excited to tell him about his new Digimon (or was it Pokemon) that he forgets to tell me goodbye. Of course he doesn't cry, he is, after all, ten years old now. But I cry. All the way home. And I ask myself, how is a mother supposed to learn that when her son leaves for camp, he will be back home soon, if she doesn't experience it first hand?

Courage is what got me through a lot of the "firsts" in my son's life, first days of school, first trips away from home, and I'm sure there will be more firsts in our lifetime. Eleanor Roosevelt said: "You gain strength, courage, and confidence by every experience in which you stop to look fear in the face." I think she had it right, but I would like to add to it by saying that courage is not only looking fear in the face, but refusing to turn-tail and run in the opposite direction! So even without the red cape, *Courage!* is my cry as I go forward.

Chapter Seven

Autism as a culture

This is important, so take a moment to consider it: Autism is
a way of being. It is not possible to separate the person from
the autism.

(Jim Sinclair, Autism Network International)

And, yes, I pray EVERY DAY for a cure to eradicate the
autism that challenges her.

*(Susan Moreno, editor and founder of MAAP
Services Inc., speaking of her daughter)*

One of the most recent controversies in the *community of autism* is the
question of whether autism should basically be considered a *disability* or
a *culture*. Once again, I can relate what I've found, but this issue, like so
many others, is up to the reader to decide.

The argument follows along these lines. If autism is a disability, then
we should help that disabled person with interventions, treatments and
eventually a cure. Autism is something that should not be in that person's
life and therefore gotten rid of. On the other hand, if autism is a culture,
then it is just a *different* way of life for that individual. As we try to tolerate
and treat every other culture with respect and understanding, we should
do the same with autism. In this case, it is the community which needs to
adjust and change, not the individual who has autism. The argument
seems pretty cut and dried when explained this way, but believe me it is
not. This chapter will probably be the briefest chapter due to the fact that
I can only scratch the surface of this issue. If you take a stand, on either
side, not only how you look at autism will be affected, but the child you
are working with will be affected too.

The first quote above is from the website of Autism Network International (ANI), where they've posted Jim Sinclair's 1993 presentation, which he gave at the International Conference in Toronto. Sinclair is addressing parents of individuals who have autism, and I would recommend you going to the site to read the entire piece. The main issue Sinclair points out is that "autism is not death" and should not be treated as an end. He states that although this is not the child who the parents expected, this is a living breathing child. He exhorts parents not to mourn for this child or for what was not, but to "explore what is" with this child.

The second quote is from Susan Moreno, parent and founder of MAAP Services (More Advanced Autistic Persons was the original name, but this has since evolved to include the complete spectrum). Moreno is expressing her thoughts about the issue of culture in her piece titled "I Wish There Were An Island." She points out that if autism were a culture and there was a perfect island for this culture, one of the main goals of course would be that neurotypicals and individuals with autism would live in perfect harmony. However, she states that since this island does not exist, she as a parent has had to try to help her daughter exist in this world. She has done this with interventions, treatments and "tons of love." Moreno states that if there were a cure for autism, she feels that it would take away her daughter's very real difficulties, not her daughter's personality.

Here are two very strong arguments, for and against. However this line is not drawn only between autistic persons and parents of autistic individuals. I have found several young adults with autism who have said they would go after a cure in the blink of an eye. I have also found several parents who wholly believe that their child's autism is who that child is, and they would not wish it away for a minute.

Not surprisingly, the question of culture doesn't begin with the autism community. This same question has existed with people dealing with deafness, and loss of sight for many years and there are several websites still debating it as an ongoing topic.

As the parents of an autistic child, which side should we be on? After closely following this debate, I have tried to stand in the middle. I have spoken several times with Jean Paul Bovee, an autistic young man who firmly believes that he cannot be separated from his autism, and wouldn't wish to be. He was also one of the speakers at the first Autism Rally in Washington, DC, and gave a very moving "I have a dream" speech about autism and acceptance. So when I read Bovee, or other writers such as Jerry Newport and Paul McDonald, both autistic individuals, I understand and agree with their argument for acceptance in the community for who they are. But I understand others' reasoning, such as Jonathan Mitchell, another individual with autism, who writes in a MAAP newsletter: "I view my own and others' autism as a horrible affliction and I wish the condition could be eradicated." Mitchell also wishes for the same respect and acceptance from the community as others do, but he sees autism as something that should be "eradicated." And of course there are many who echo Mitchell and Susan Moreno's words. DAN, Defeat Autism Now, is one such organization, and I regularly read everything that they contribute to the autism community. However, I must admit that on this issue, I am on the fence. But is this such a bad place to be? Can one function from this position?

At our recent IEP meeting we began planning for seventh grade. In sixth grade Jon's personal aide (para) was taken away and he was in a regular classroom which was an *inclusion* setting. This inclusion classroom was where the teacher has five other students with IEPs who have special needs mixed into the regular classroom. A second teacher comes into in the classroom to "team" teach a few of the subjects, and to give extra support to these five students. At the beginning of the year this change was very stressful for Jon and we had more bad days and weeks than good. However, as the year progressed things have gotten calmer. Jon has learned some independence and is still succeeding, at least academically, in the regular classroom. But when it came time to plan for next year, his two teachers and I came to the realization separately that Jon will probably benefit in having a para again for the seventh grade. Not only is seventh grade too different from sixth grade, but it will be a different school, with a different staff, and seven different teachers changing every hour. As a result, we have set goals that he will have a para who will be more of a tutor and not a shadow. This person will be someone to make sure he is on task, give extra explanation on work if needed, and be a valuable support for those seven teachers in working with Jon. So once again, in seventh grade, we will be doing a tightrope act. We will be trying to balance between learning independence and appropriate social behavior, with having necessary support close by to be able to function in the mainstream of life. We will continue to challenge him, push him to succeed, but with the understanding that he will need extra supports in place. We will continue to *modify* his *behavior* but we want to *TEACCH* him in a way that he can learn. (Both, you notice, are two different methods of intervention. We straddle that line too!)

So, is autism a culture or a disability? You will need to decide, but don't be ashamed to straddle the fence. As long as you are trying to do what is best for your child, why worry if someone accuses you of being a fence-sitter? Respecting both sides of the issue is what I believe is important.

References

Mitchell, J. (2001) "Letters to the Editor." *The MAAP 4*, 7.

Moreno, S. (2001) "I Wish There Were An Island." The *MAAP 3*, 4–5.

Sinclair, J. (2000) "Don't Mourn For Us." ANI online posting, 29 November
    ani.autistics.org/dont_mourn.html (2001, 20 September).

chicken nugget #7

Forgiving others—forgiving ourselves

True forgiveness is up to God. But I can forget.

(Anonymous)

Women and elephants never forget an injury!

(Hector Hugh Monro, 1870–1916)

I think the truth about forgiveness lies somewhere between these two quotes. I had actually almost forgotten about the taekwondo instructor who had made my son cry (in Nugget #2). I do still wonder if I should have gone back and explained things to her once again, to try to make the situation work. But I feel that if I constantly go back to explain things to every person who in my eyes may have wronged my son, I will spend a majority of my life going backwards instead of forwards. Most people usually act out of lack of information or ignorance of the situation. It's not as if they intended to hurt my child.

I remember one such situation when my son attended our after-school care program. It seemed that my son had an internal clock, because usually when I arrived to pick him up he was waiting for me at the door with his arms spread wide. One day as I got to the door, a very angry woman came out. She was looking over her shoulder and was saying "How rude!" I looked inside and saw my son standing in front of the door. He hurried towards me to give me a hug. This woman stopped for a moment and added, "I mean, he's standing right there, and he wouldn't even move out of the way. I never saw a child so rude!" Well, I had never seen a parent so angry about something that seemed so trivial to me. I quickly pulled out of my son's embrace and turned him to face her. He was totally oblivious to what had transpired. I explained to him what she had said, and told him that he needed to apologize for standing in her way. He blinked his eyes and looked up at her. "Oh, I didn't even see her," he said. She grasped her child's hand, and, without another word, pulled him towards the car. When my son realized how angry she was, he became upset. I patted him on the shoulder, explained to him that he couldn't stand right in front of the doors and wait for me any more, and also that this mom was probably having a bad day.

After this incident, I had two options. I could forget the entire thing, or the next time I saw this mom I could explain about my son and his autism and that he really wasn't aware that she was trying to get out the door. I chose to forget this one. True, it would have taken just a minute to speak to her, but I didn't want to get into the habit of going backwards.

My husband has had to make similar choices. One fall the local newspaper was doing a segment on "Parents with Children with Disabilities and Working with the Schools." I was asked to write a short piece on our child, and it ran next to a superintendent's piece on what he thought was "too much" spending on "these" children. After the series was in the paper, my husband was at a community business meeting. A total stranger approached him and said, "I read your wife's article in the paper. I just want you to know how very sorry I am for your situation, and that it must be horrible for you with your autistic child!" My husband told me that his mouth dropped open, and he was at a total loss for words. He stood for a moment as she went on to give her condolences. Finally, he found his voice, and he told her pointblank, "I don't want to talk about this right now," turned and walked away. Yes, this woman's intentions were probably good, but it was the wrong place, the wrong thing to say, and my husband didn't even know her.

I remember my husband being very angry as he told me about this. Who was this woman to approach him during a business meeting and give him sympathy? Pity? Both emotions made him angry since he felt that as a family we didn't need either. It also made him angry that a total stranger had gained this "access" to our family from a simple newspaper article. What could we do about this situation to make sure that it never happened again? I began writing under a pen name to protect the privacy of my family. Yes, there are many well-informed and supportive people in the world, but there are a lot of uninformed people too. No matter how much information is disseminated about autism, there will always be someone making a verbal blunder, or possibly misunderstanding my son. I gladly leave the serious forgiving up to God and try not to be like the elephant with forgetting!

Forgiving ourselves

> This one thing I do, forgetting those things which are behind, and reaching forth unto those things which are before, I press toward the mark.
>
> *(Philippians 3:13–14)*

If we try to keep a record of all of the mistakes that we may have made in our lifetime, the list would be too cumbersome to carry. Everyone makes mistakes. And how many times have we heard that! Paul is telling the Philippians two things in this quote, to forget those things that are past, and to keep pressing on towards our goal.

So when it comes to ourselves, how do we do this? There are numerous books on forgiveness, and there are probably very practical step-by-step programs on self-forgiveness. Like so many other areas, everyone truly needs to find his or her own way. I don't know if forgiveness is more difficult for a parent of a child with special needs, but I do know that dwelling on past mistakes is sometimes unbearable.

I try to forget the time when my son was an infant and after many sleepless nights was lying in his crib crying for apparently no reason. Everything had been checked and double-checked. He was diapered, fed, not ill that I could see, but still crying uncontrollably at 3:00 in the morning. What did I do? I stood by his crib and yelled back "Just what do you want?" Of course I immediately felt remorse. He couldn't answer, for goodness sake, he was a baby! I gently picked him up and took him downstairs. After I placed him in his swing and wound it up he stopped crying, and it was my turn to shed the tears. What good was yelling at him? He didn't know why he was crying. (Like I said, I try to forget that one, but as one can see, it is still there!).

Why is it that we can't seem to forget, when it comes to forgetting and forgiving ourselves? Do we really believe that because our children have special needs we need to be perfect parents to them?

After my son's diagnosis I remember a time when we were walking into the local library. Jon had never had what you would call a "normal" gait, and when he was younger his odd way of walking was very noticeable (still is actually). It was a hot summer day, there was a lot of traffic, and I was trying to grab hold of his flailing hand. I finally stopped and, taking his hand, said, "Would you just walk normal, please!" This request, to an autistic child! What I really wanted was for him to calm down and take my hand so that we could cross the street. A slip of the tongue, and I still remember my instant feelings of guilt. What a thing to say to my own child. He didn't understand my request any more than I understood where it had come from.

We crossed the street, and when we got in front of the library he wanted to explore the small rock garden at the entrance. This was fine. I needed some calming down time myself. I remember sitting on a bench and looking at all the rocks at my feet. My son was checking out a worm or bug he had found. I leaned over and picked up a rock that was the size and shape of a small pickle, smooth and warm to the touch. Suddenly I wondered how long it took to get all of the rough edges smoothed off, to get it shaped like a pickle. Then I had one of those moments—a ping of understanding. It took a long time to shape this rock, just like it was going to take a long time to shape my son and me. Yes, sometimes we rub up against each other, but we are both a work in progress. I never hold grudges or remember my son's past mistakes. Why couldn't I learn to forgive and forget my own? I put that rock in my pocket, took my son's hand, and we happily went into the library.

I still have that rock, along with a small pile that he and I have picked up over the years. It's nice to look at them and remember the day I learned a lesson in forgiving myself. We are so understanding with our children, sometimes we need to remember to be just as understanding with ourselves. Because I for one don't want to be associated with that non-forgiving elephant!

Chapter Eight

What do Aristotle and autism have in common?

No, Aristotle wasn't thought to be autistic, although some think a few of our great thinkers, for example Einstein, were perhaps autistic or had Asperger's Syndrome. Look into it yourself. You will be amazed! On the contrary, the link I wish to point out in this chapter is *ethical rhetoric* and *writing* about autism. In Aristotle's work, *The Art of Rhetoric*, he devotes one entire section on how to use rhetoric, or language, in order to "impress the hearers and influence them for or against a certain course of action." He breaks this down by defining three ways (he calls them appeals) in which people (in Aristotle's case public speakers, in our case writers) use language to persuade. The first is *ethos*, which refers to the character or reputation of the writer. If you are reading a book, and you know up front that the author has a good reputation or credentials, the ethos of that writer works in the writer's behalf to persuade the reader. Another, *pathos*, is when the writer plays on the emotions of the reader (pushes their hot buttons) to persuade them, and these emotions could be positive or negative. The last is *logos*, which is not necessarily the use of facts in the writing, but a logical progression which succeeds in convincing the reader of fact. Most speakers and writers are very aware of these three appeals, but we as readers are not, and this is where I see the connection to autism.

Any writer is using rhetoric, or language, to write about this very important subject—autism. Anything you read is using some type of appeal to persuade you that this information is the truth. But if the writer is using poor judgment in their writing, by possibly misusing one of these appeals, you the reader may be negatively affected and more importantly, your child will be affected too.

My goal in this chapter is to give you a mini-lesson on rhetoric and show by example how each of these—ethos, pathos and logos—are used (or possibly misused). As I stated at the opening of this book, I believe knowledge brings power. Why shouldn't you, as a reader, understand how language itself is being used to affect you? Oliver Wendell Holmes, Sr., physician and poet, is attributed with saying that "man's mind stretched to a new idea never goes back to its original dimensions." My goal for you after this chapter is to never *read* the same again.

A short note about disclaimers and responsibility

In addition to the fact that every writer uses some type of appeal (ethos, pathos, logos) to persuade, every writer usually uses a disclaimer. How many of us have gotten used to reading something along these lines—the information contained within is for informational purposes only and is not to be used without consulting a professional—that we hardly pay any attention to them at all. (You will notice I had to put one at the front of this book too.) This disclaimer supposedly relieves the writer of responsibility, just in case anything adverse happens as a result of their words. But does this mean that they are relieved of the task of writing about their subject ethically? Or course not. It is still the writer's responsibility not only to choose their words carefully, but to choose how they use these words.

A writer of any piece is asking the reader to believe, rely on, agree with or accept in some way their ideas. If this idea has to do with a life-affecting issue such as autism, then the writer needs to be doubly responsible. Disclaimer or not, writers must be aware of the power of their words, and they must endeavor to write ethically.

Writing about medical topics

Very little is written about the *rhetoric* of medical writing. It's as if there is a wall built around this field, protecting it from any deep analysis. But if rhetoric is what is used in every piece of writing, and medical writing is giving information on a particular subject, then ethos, pathos or logos is being used, even in medical writing, to persuade.

In fact, sometimes it is the rhetoric used in medical writing which can become more important than the information itself. Judy Segal is one of the researchers who has looked at the use of rhetoric in medical writing. In "Strategies of Influence in Medical Authorship," Segal (1993a) points out how important it is for medical writers to convince the reader about the truth of their information. The most obvious reason is "competition within the profession" and Segal explains that to get an article published is a very difficult task. Writers are reviewed by an editorial staff, no matter if it is for a journal or a publishing house. Thus, right up front, rhetoric is used by the writer to gain admittance to publication. After publication, Segal states that not surprisingly the "reputation of the author depends on [the article's] reception within the professional community" (p.522). Hence, rhetoric again plays an important role in convincing readers that the writer's information is important, true, and perhaps even revolutionary. If writers fail to convince either at the beginning of the process, or later after publication, it is possible that their medical writing will have been for nothing. Not only is there a chance that they will not be published, but if they are published they may quickly be forgotten, or worse discredited. Hence, there are very high stakes in medical writing. You not only have writers wanting to and needing to be published, but you also have a readership who will possibly act on the writers' words.

A way with words

The caution to "choose your words carefully" could never be more important than in medical writing. In discussing the *style* of medical writing, Segal points out several ways that medical writers use words. These writers include the use of passive voice in their reports (it was found), use qualifiers (it is theorized), and base the entire article on a question or dialogue (is the use of type A or type B drug a benefit?) (1993a, pp.526–528). The result is that the reader feels the report holds more weight because "it was found." So the writer covers himself by stating something was theorized and with the use of question and answer, the question itself is not scrutinized, if either drug A or B will in fact benefit. (This reminds me of when we used to ask our parents if we could have a party. We would say "For my birthday can I have 30 or 12 kids over?" Our parents usually reacted immediately by protesting, "Oh, no! Only 12 kids please!" Thus, the question of if we could have a party was not even discussed!)

Along these same lines, in *The Ethics of Rhetoric*, Richard Weaver (1953) boils it down to choice of terms. He believes that "all of the terms in a rhetorical vocabulary are like links in a chain stretching up to some master link which transmits its influence" (p.23). Thus, as writers choose their terminology, they create a chain. To Weaver, "rhetoric, noble or base, is a great power in the world" and he points out repeatedly that a speaker or writer must constantly check and re-check not only his/her words, but the *effect* of those words as well. Once a writer's words are set on paper, if only one person reads them there will be an effect. And it is this effect which writers need to be constantly aware of during the process of choosing their words and "creating this chain."

Beginning with ethos—who is this writer?

I must admit that it was an article that made me look more closely at rhetoric. Remember ethos is the character or reputation of the writer, or the character or reputation infused into the words of the writer. If writers don't bring ethos to their writing by who they are, then they need to produce ethos in their writing by what they say.

Soon after my son was diagnosed, I received a phone call from a friend. She had been in the doctor's office and found a magazine article titled something along the lines of "Cured of Autism!" She thought I should read the article immediately. She wanted me to go out and try to find the magazine as soon as I could so that I could look into this for my own son. After hanging up the phone, I called the local ACCESS office (Project Access) and repeated my phone conversation. Yes, the woman at ACCESS said. They had been getting numerous phone calls about this article. In fact she had a copy of it hanging in her office and would fax it to me. She then added that, no, they had not found a cure for autism, and that I should read the article myself and make my own judgments.

When the article came, I did just that. What I found was one family's story about taking their son off certain food products, and how they believed he was no longer autistic. Did this writer have any ethos to be making this claim? This was a parent, just as I was, but they were not in the medical or nutritional field. Did the writer infuse his/her words with ethos by using logos, a logical progression of information which resulted in fact? The writer quoted two sources to support his/her claims, both of them out of the country and not supported by our FDA yet. And did this writer use pathos in the article to perhaps play on the reader's emotions? I would think the gripping title of the article referring to a cure for autism answers that question. (I do realize that the title may have been the editorial staff's choice.)

Of course this writer had a disclaimer. He/she warned others to check with their physician. But this disclaimer did not negate all of the confusion and false hope that occurred in printing this article.

Everyone comes with ethos (who they are). The writer of this article's ethos was that of a parent, dealing with what happened in their family with their child. The problem, I feel, happened when the information in the article got blown out of proportion, quoted inaccurately, or taken, just as the title suggested, as a cure for autism. When writers forget their own ethos, it becomes our responsibility as readers to remember who we are reading. Yes, that parent is an expert, but only in the telling of their story and their child, nothing else.

Professionals have a head start

Professional organizations as well as professionals in the field bring a completely different type of ethos to their writing. The Autism Society of America (ASA) has been in existence since the 1960s, and was originally founded by a group of parents of children with autism. These parents brought their parental ethos together when they formed this group, and in the last 30 years this parental ethos has evolved to a professional level. This professional ethos is not only connected to years of experience, but also to a track record for producing work that carries ethos. Because of ASA's high standards in regard to what they will or will not publish, and the style in which they write, they have created their ethos. The organization's underlying goal is to further the knowledge of education concerning autism, autism research, and to provide necessary support to the autistic community. In their newsletter, *The Advocate*, one finds professionals writing on research and therapies, side by side with personal, family accounts about autism. As a result, there are no tabloid headlines about cures or treatments, but instead page after page of documented, supportable information. Even when they do an issue on current causes, cures or treatments, it is done not only with the all-important disclaimer, but also the statement that as yet there is no known cause or cure for autism, and that some of the treatments listed herein are not clinically proven. In addition, this same ethos can be found on their website. Thus, by carefully choosing their words in all of their work, they have responsibly built their ethos.

Similar to organizations, professionals in the field of autism bring a very different ethos to their writing. Dr. Temple Grandin is one such professional. She is an individual who is not only high functioning autistic, but has earned a PhD in science and is reported as "our nation's most expert designer of humane facilities for livestock animals" ("Inventor of the Week," MIT website). Hence, Grandin's ethos is multi-layered.

Along with her years of experience (she is in her fifties), she is scientifically trained and autistic herself. In her book *Thinking in Pictures*, Grandin (1995) clearly uses the writing style of a professional. Not only does she use qualifiers in her writing where necessary, but one can also see that she chooses her words carefully. In a chapter where she discusses behaviors and causes of autism, she uses words such as "it *appears*" and "autistics *sometimes*" or "*some* parents suspect" (pp.52–59). But when stating facts she drops all qualifiers and states for example that "research has very clearly shown that autism is a neurological disorder that reveals distinct abnormalities in the brain" (p.50). When she discusses the many "theories" about the cause of autism and numerous "methods of treatment," she rightly concludes that no treatment is 100 percent right for every autistic individual. As a result, she infuses ethos into her work by her writing style, choice of words, and several practical personal notes, such as when she writes that "a neurologist gave my mother some very good advice: to follow her own instincts" (p.57). Grandin states that it is the parents who are with the child 24 hours a day and know the child intimately; therefore, the parents should trust themselves. She also points out that "parents who are desperate to reach their autistic children often look for miracles" and she believes that parents get caught up in this search out of the love for their child (p.58). Does she condemn parents for this search? No. She is only attempting to explain why parents do this. But, by discussing it, along with many other "touchy" issues, she not only shows her professionalism, but infuses her words with ethos.

Is pathos appropriate?

Pathos is the appeal that engages the reader's feelings of sympathy, empathy, sadness and joy or anger. It is what causes a close connection between the writer and the reader. Thus, it also has the ability to push the reader's "hot buttons." Segal states that "direct emotional appeals are unconventional in medicine. Nevertheless, one powerful means of persuasion lies in the formation of an alliance between author and audience" (1993a, p.524). She explains that the way this alliance works in medical writing is when writers dissociate themselves from the subject of the article. Many times writers refer to the *subject* or *patient* of the article as "they," and the "we" in the article is the *writer* and *reader* combined. By doing this, the reader feels a strong connection with the writer, not with the subject of the article. Thus, in a very subtle way the writer has immediately engaged the passions, and gained the support of the reader.

Weaver (1953) also discusses pathos in reference to scientists. He states that "if one's writing is abstract, it will accommodate ideas, but it will fatigue the reader. If it is concrete, it will divert and relieve; but it may become cloying, and it will have difficulty in encompassing ideas" (p.209). Therefore, he explains, the writer of science needs to understand this and realize that their writing is going to be "purely descriptive" and that "not many people are going to develop a sense of poignant concern over such a presentation" (p.209). To Weaver, it is the science writer's duty to impart the facts in as understandable a language as possible so that "[the writing] is expression with a definite assignment of duty" (p.208). He concludes that if science writers have not been responsible in their use of rhetoric, a possible problem occurs when the writer's "means seem to manipulate ends" (p.210). In other words, the writer has put forth the information, engaged the reader's passions, but the way the information is presented has manipulated the end, as opposed to the information itself leading to conclusion. Thus, the reader has become emotionally involved in the article, with a result that all information in the article is easily accepted. This condition, Weaver warns, "is one which science, along with every other instrumentality of education, should be combating in the interest of a reasonable world" (p.210).

The pathos of parents

When parents are writing about their own children, can they write without pathos? They can if they realize that they are writing about a medical subject. Just as it is necessary to realize what ethos they have or ought to infuse in their work, they also need to decide if pathos is appropriate in their work, and if it is, how much? Balance is the key.

In Charles Hart's (1993) book, *A Parent's Guide to Autism*, Hart is not only the father of an autistic child, but he grew up with an autistic older brother who was born in the 1920s, a time when this disorder was not yet diagnosed and grossly misunderstood. The introduction to this book is where Hart uses the appeal of pathos as we learn about his brother and his son. Here he uses a style of writing that immediately connects with the reader and engages the feelings. The last lines of this introduction read: "Ask yourself: What would I do if I couldn't express myself through words? How could I learn if the teacher's sounds didn't seem to match the gestures?" He then explains that "this book encourages you to ask many questions. Readers who ask the right questions will make better choices for their daughters and sons with autism" (p.3). The reader is immediately pulled into this dialogue, question and answer, and has established a connection with the writer.

Although Hart hooks the reader with pathos in his introduction, it seems that he senses his responsibility in the body of his book. After the introduction, the book reads as a non-emotional resource book. Each chapter is headed with questions ranging from "Is autism caused by parents and could they have done anything to prevent it?" to "Should you believe in miracles?" Hart has an opportunity to infuse his answers with pathos. After all, the questions themselves push the reader's emotional hot buttons, but he refrains from doing so. He does what Segal suggests medical writers should do, in that although he is a parent he dissociates himself from the subject. As a parent, he probably pondered every single one of these questions, but he doesn't talk about that. Each question is discussed in a textbook-like manner. He gives the facts, quotes his sources, answers common objections, and then gives a review of the information at the end of each chapter.

His conclusion is another place where pathos could be infused, by grasping the reader with an anecdote or more personal information at the end, but Hart resists doing even this. His last paragraph states that "we need to make the most of available therapies, to abandon those that are useless, and promote those with proven value. Then parents will find it easier to raise a child with autism" (p.226). He chooses not to push hot buttons, not to play on the reader's emotions to ensure believability. Hart's work, in Weaver's terms, could be described as "purely descriptive." But contrary to what Weaver suggests, the reader does develop a "sense of…concern" with the work because as a parent Hart responsibly finds the right balance of pathos to infuse in his work, which of course results in producing more of his own ethos.

Professionals and pathos

Professional organizations and professionals in any field must be cautious when it comes to using pathos as a tool. Because of the ethos they bring to their writing, they already have a connection with the reader and their words are going to be accepted more readily. In a sense, they have an easier job set before them because of who they are. Thus, is it appropriate for a professional organization or professional in the field to infuse their work with pathos in trying to connect with the reader emotionally? Segal points out that when the writers of medical articles do not distance themselves from the subject, but connect closely with it, the articles are somehow discredited and not read as science (1993a, p.524).

So, how then does an organization like the ASA use pathos? Does it at all? Is it appropriate for them to try to connect emotionally with their readers? The ASA is a not-for-profit organization. It has grown from a small parent support group in the 1960s to an international organization that has approximately 24,000 members. They offer a fax-on-demand service, and an information department that handles approximately 15,000 calls a day and distributes 30,000 information packets a year. How do they fund such a venture? Entirely through membership donations, fund raisers, and gifts. Hence, here is where the ASA uses pathos in their work. They do a mailing quarterly to update the community on autism. This mailing is in the form of a short letter and has as the logo a silhouette of a child looking downward, imposed on top of puzzle pieces (the puzzle meaning they are fitting together the pieces of autism, and how best to help). If this doesn't grab the reader, the envelope they send to mail a donation in will. Here is a picture of a small boy on the back of the envelope. He is looking straight at the reader. He is not smiling or frowning; he just *is*. One wonders how they captured it on film, because this is what autism is—the face of this boy. Boatloads of pathos in one small picture. This then is one of the places you will find pathos used by the ASA, but can we blame them? They are trying to raise money for a good cause. They need to connect with the reader. They need to push some hot buttons or they will not be funded. No blame is leveled because once again balance is the key.

The pathos in Dr. Grandin's book, similar to Hart's, is mainly in the introduction. But the introduction is not written by the author, it is written by the famous neurologist, Oliver Sacks (1995a). He spent time with Grandin and got to know her when he was writing his book *An*

Anthropologist on Mars (1995b). (Its title comes from Grandin who told Sacks that this is how she feels in society.) One of the major areas of difficulty for people with autism is emotions. Consequently, in this instance the pathos used to engage the reader is derived from someone else. Sacks gives a short biographical essay about Grandin and ends by telling us about their drive back to the airport after interviewing her. He says that as they are talking, Grandin suddenly wept and said, "I don't want my thoughts to die with me. I want to have done something...I want to know that my life has meaning" (Sacks 1995a, p.15). The reader realizes that this is why Grandin is writing this book: to try to explain autism from the inside out, not only to help others understand it, but so that her thoughts will not die with her.

If Sacks hadn't engaged the reader with pathos in his introduction, would Grandin have been able to do so herself? It is hard to say. But for someone who is supposed to be lacking in emotion because of autism, Grandin does succeed in interspersing pathos into her writing. Mixed in with the information on her thought processes, her description of her work with animals and slaughterhouses, and her sometimes scientific terminology, pathos is felt. The writing has a few snags, perhaps due to Grandin's different way of processing thought, and sometimes it is hard to figure out exactly what she is trying to say. But perhaps it is this slight awkwardness that causes the reader to connect with the work. As the reader begins to understand the information that people with autism think differently, they also feel the differences in Grandin's style of writing. Thus, by the book's conclusion, the reader is not only better informed about autism, but they have a feeling that they now know Grandin personally, and can relate to her difficulties in thinking. Segal's warning comes to mind that if a medical writer connects too closely with a work, it will lack credibility. She is right in one sense. Because of Grandin's close connection to her subject, her work is not read as science. But this in no way discredits the work as Segal suggests it would. Grandin's work is very credible, and for someone who is supposed to be lacking in pathos, Grandin succeeds in finding the right mix.

The foundation of logos

If any of the three rhetorical appeals could be called the foundation of medical writing, it would be logos. Logos is the appearance of a logical process in the work that convinces the reader of fact. Of course, convincing the reader of fact is the main goal of medical writing. Once the reader is convinced, then the reader proceeds to the next goal of medical writing which is to change the reader's thinking on the subject. Once the thinking has changed, the final goal is action. The reader acts according to what is read. Hence, a great responsibility rests on the writer's shoulders. Logos not only needs to be evident in the work, but it needs to be accurate.

In "Writing and Medicine," Segal (1993b) looks at the style of an article written on headaches and states that "the appeal from ethos may, in fact, carry a medical journal article when the appeal from scientific logos fails" (p.88). She explains that in this study, when the researcher's numbers on headaches were closely examined, the figures didn't add up. When looked at closely, it was discovered that the researchers used only two different treatments on 16 women who suffered from only four different headache conditions (p.89). Because of the ethos of the paper, this lack of support in the research had somehow not been noticed, when in reality the writers lacked logos. However, the article was published, and it wasn't until the figures were closely examined that the problem with lack of research was discovered.

In addition, Segal describes several ways in which logos is used in medical writing; one being what Aristotle called "inartistic proofs"—proofs that are not from the writer but have been established beforehand. In science writing, these are the references that the writer makes to others' work (1993a, p.524). These other works then become a main part of the foundation of logos that the writer is building.

However, as Segal points out, even citing another's work can be misused. She states that "the principle of *selective* citation has an important pragmatic function: authors could not possibly cite every source. ... Still, what is selected is often a matter of what *best supports* the case at hand (1993a, p.524, my emphasis). In other words, the citations may be accurate and truthful, but they are only what supports the writer's views. This is where the ethos of the writer connects with the logos. If the writer is someone of good character (ethos) and they wish their work to carry that ethos, they will cite not only what supports their views, but also things that contradict them. Then it becomes part of the writer's job to try to refute those contradictions.

This style of logical argument, "citing and refuting," Segal refers to as "Blanton's shifts." Blanton, as quoted by Segal, states that most articles are "designed to guide the reader's attention and thought through the development shifts of: AGREED, BUT, BUT SUPPOSE, THEN, INDEED" (1993a, p.526). According to Segal, this is a responsible logical process of a medical article.

Along these same lines, Weaver states that "dialectic is that stage which defines the subject satisfactorily with regard to the logos" (1953, p.27). To Weaver, dialectics (a back and forth discussion) is the way to establish all logos. It disputes established or admitted facts, and to do this successfully one must suspend the argument until the facts are settled.

Professionalism's necessary foundation

Dr. Grandin, a PhD recipient and scientist, seems to understand better than anyone the importance of logos. In fact, at times her book reads like a textbook as each chapter lays down information in a logical process. Grandin makes her point, supports her point by either citing someone in the field or from personal experience (depending on the topic) and concludes her point. The writer does not feel that Grandin is selectively citing because she cites several treatments and theories about autism that she also questions and disagrees with. But like a true professional she doesn't shy away from giving her opinion on the subject. In several chapters, Blanton's shifts—agreed, but, but suppose, then, indeed—can be seen. Thus, she successfully uses logical process. The argument of whether people with autism do indeed think differently is temporarily set aside, as Weaver suggests, until all of the facts are settled. As a result, by the end of the work, the reader is convinced that they have undeniably read the truth, and that autistics do think differently.

The ASA, as a professional organization, intrinsically understands that logos is necessary for its continuance. In every issue of *The Advocate* there is a page containing the "ASA and Advocate Statements and Policies." This is different from a disclaimer in that this is a policy statement explaining that the group supports "active and informed involvement of family members and the individual with autism in the planning of individualized, appropriate services and supports" (ASA 2000, p.4). The group states that not every program fulfills every individual's needs and that all services should be based solely on a positive effect on the individual (p.4). In fact they are stating what type of information they will publish in their newsletter, on their website, and allow at their conventions: "high-quality information in a variety of fields to meet the needs of ASA's members" (p.4). If material doesn't meet this high standard, it isn't published or posted.

It is this attempt, a strict adherence to logos in all information, that has created ASA's ethos. When there are instances of questionable information, then the ASA prints a warning along with the information such as the one on their website about autism and diet: "This listing of resources is given on an information only basis. It is not to be construed as an endorsement by the Autism Society of America". The reader realizes that the ASA has set themselves up as watchdogs in the autism community, and they do not take this responsibility lightly.

Parents and the facts

Any parent who is writing on the subject of autism has a decision to make before they ever begin their work. Of course they need to be very careful to make sure that their work contains the proper amount of logos, correctly cited and defended. But in addition they need to decide if they are willing to concede that they are a parent, not a professional, in the field of autism, and therefore write about what they know only from personal experience.

Again, Charles Hart (1993) very successfully handles this decision by becoming a very talented compiler of information, and the secret to his success lies in his "inartistic" proofs. Hart squeezes into a 244-page book enough information on autism that someone else might put into five books. Determined that his book should be a resource on autism, he leaves out a lot of pathos and anecdotal information, and does what he has set out to do: answer readers' questions. Not only does he correctly cite known information (his inartistic proofs), he cites information that he himself may disagree with. Then he proceeds to cite again, to explain why he disagrees. He uses Blanton's shifts to do this, and it is as if he has studied the technique. Hart's last chapter titled "Where Can Parents Get More Information?" lists organizations, books by parents, books by autistics and foundations. In this last chapter is a perfect example of Hart's logos for not only does he list information that he agrees with, but information that he does not. He has stayed true to his job of compiler by putting together a list for readers to locate information and judge for themselves. There is no argument being settled in his book, or with his book, and the reader comes away fully convinced that Hart has reported the facts. Yes, he is a parent and not a professional in the field, but because he has done such a good job of citing and compiling, his book is a success.

Final thoughts on responsibility

It is my wish for writers of an article, book, newsletter or website on autism to keep these points in mind:

1. Know who you are, or, who you are not, and write accordingly. Ethos.

2. Realize your subject matter, and understand if pushing people's hot buttons is appropriate. Pathos.

3. Understand the importance of writing about the subject in an accurate and logical way. Logos.

If these are remembered, one should be able to write responsibly on any subject, without irresponsibly encouraging someone to act upon their words, with possible negative results.

Most importantly you, as a reader, need to keep these same guidelines in mind. Now you have the knowledge to look more closely at anything you are reading, on any subject—beginning with the one in your hand. Notice what the writer's *ethos* is. Realize when they are using *pathos*, and try to track the *logos* within the information. If you do this, you should never be taken advantage of as you seek information, and you will be able to make a more informed decision about your child. Once again remember that we need to be optimistic about our children, but we also need to have a good dose of pessimism to balance things out. Be an *informed* reader.

References

Autism Society of America (ASA) "Autism and Diet." www.autism-society.org (2001, 11 June)

Autism Society of America (ASA) (2000) *The Advocate 33*, cover page.

Grandin, T. (1995) *Thinking in Pictures: And Other Reports from my Life with Autism.* New York: Doubleday.

Hart, C. (1993) *A Parent's Guide to Autism.* New York: Pocket Books.

Sacks, O. (1995a) "Introduction." In T. Grandin *Thinking in Pictures: And Other Reports from my Life with Autism.* New York: Doubleday.

Sacks, O. (1995b) *An Anthropologist on Mars.* New York: Knopf.

Segal, J.Z. (1993a) "Strategies of Influence in Medical Authorship." *Social Science of Medicine 37*, 521–530.

Segal, J.Z. (1993b) "Writing and Medicine." In R. Spilka (ed) *Writing in the Workplace: New Research Perspectives.* Carbondale and Edwardsville, IL: Southern Illinois University Press, pp.84–97.

Weaver, R.M. (1953) *The Ethics of Rhetoric.* Chicago: Henry Regnery.

chicken nugget #8

Would you like sauce with those nuggets?

Sauce? Sauce is what you dunk your nugget in to help it go down. If you didn't have the sauce, the nugget may be more difficult to swallow. In my son's case it was a dunk of ketchup with every bite, but you get the idea. No matter how healthy that "nugget" may be for you, sometimes you have to have the sauce to help. No matter how important the information in this book may be, you may need that extra something to take it all in. Thus, what follows is just that: a little added extra.

1. *Remember: you are not alone.* This is MAAP's battlecry and has become mine too. You do not have to go it alone, fight your battles alone, or research your child's situation alone. Please take advantage of the network of people and organizations that are out there for you. Don't hesitate to call a total stranger and unburden yourself. I did, and I found that we were *related* by autism.

2. *You are not only a parent, you are your child's advocate.* No one else will care for or fight for your child like you will. No one else will be able to get the services for your child like you will. Realize both of these facts and become an *educated* and *armed* parent advocate. Try not to go into any IEP meeting unprepared. Don't sign anything that you don't agree with or don't understand. And don't worry if they think you are the "parent from hell." It is your child's life and well-being that are at stake. You can't fight or love too much.

3. *Go with your gut instincts.* You are with your child 24 hours a day, 7 days a week. If it doesn't *feel* right, find out why. Yes, they have to listen to you. You are the parent.

4. *Try to enjoy the journey.* Happiness is really not the destination you know. Yes, we are all aiming towards goals for our children, but as in any child's life, enjoy *this* journey with your child. If you focus too much on goals, or hopeful future successes, you may miss something really special happening at that very moment. Daily, my son makes me laugh. I told him just this week that I was going to visit my sister because "mom needs a break." He took my arm and said, "Break? I'll give you a break." Then in the next breath he moaned, "Oh no. I'll be stuck with Dad forever." Ha! Take time to enjoy your own child's uniqueness now, today. They will change so quickly.

I hope that you have found some help in the book you are holding in your hand, and remember: *you can be the difference in your child's life.* Thus, from *parent to parent*—go and do, and read much, much more. The knowledge will bring you peace.

Subject index

Name index